Praise for *The Brand IDEA*

"*The Brand IDEA* is an insightful articulation of the centrality of brand and brand management in the nonprofit sector. Any organization that depends on partnerships, stakeholders, governments, employees, donors or any other type of relationship, should manage its brand proactively. *The Brand IDEA* is a much-needed and valuable resource for all who work in the nonprofit sector."
—Rob Garris, managing director, Rockefeller Foundation

"Strategic and thoughtful, this work establishes a provocative branding framework for nonprofit organizations in a challenging social media world. It makes the powerful case, and offers a clear road map, for identity alignment that is stakeholder-centered and mission-driven."
—Ray Offenheiser, president, Oxfam America

"Rich with examples from a multitude of nonprofit organizations, the authors make a profound case for why *brand* is integrally linked with the nonprofit mission. Turn to Chapter 8 for practical tools to build a strong brand and manage your brand integrity, democracy and affinity (IDEA) on behalf of your organization. It's an important resource for any nonprofit manager."
—Tanya Giovacchini, partner, chief engagement and marketing officer, The Bridgespan Group

For more testimonials and information visit
www.nonprofitbrandidea.com

THE BRAND IDEA

Managing Nonprofit Brands with Integrity, Democracy, and Affinity

**NATHALIE LAIDLER-KYLANDER
AND JULIA SHEPARD STENZEL**

Foreword by Christopher Stone, president, Open Society Foundations

JB JOSSEY-BASS™
A Wiley Brand

Published by Jossey-Bass
A Wiley Brand
One Montgomery Street, Suite 1200, San Francisco, CA 94104-4594—www.josseybass.com

Jossey-Bass books and products are available through most bookstores. To contact Jossey-Bass directly call our Customer Care Department within the U.S. at 800-956-7739, outside the U.S. at 317-572-3986, or fax 317-572-4002.

Wiley publishes in a variety of print and electronic formats and by print-on-demand. Some material included with standard print versions of this book may not be included in e-books or in print-on-demand. If this book refers to media such as a CD or DVD that is not included in the version you purchased, you may download this material at http://booksupport.wiley.com. For more information about Wiley products, visit www.wiley.com.

Library of Congress Cataloging-in-Publication Data

Laidler-Kylander, Nathalie.
  The brand IDEA : managing nonprofit brands with integrity, democracy, and affinity / Nathalie Laidler-Kylander, Julia Shepard Stenzel. —First edition.
      pages cm
  Includes bibliographical references and index.
ISBN 978-1-118-55583-5 (cloth); ISBN 978-1-118-57330-3 (ebk);
ISBN 978-1-118-57340-2 (ebk)
  1. Nonprofit organizations—Management. 2. Nonprofit organizations—Marketing.
I. Stenzel, Julia Shepard. II. Title.
HD62.6.L35 2013
658'.048—dc23
                            2013030361

Printed in the United States of America
FIRST EDITION

HB Printing   10 9 8 7 6 5 4 3 2 1

CONTENTS

PART 3:   PUTTING THE BRAND IDEA INTO ACTION

LIST OF FIGURES, TABLES, AND EXHIBITS

FOREWORD

This book stands at the intersection of several debates animating the nonprofit sector around the world. Among them: should nonprofit organizations spend precious charitable funds on managing their brands, or are those expenses wasteful vanity? Does the rise of social media mean that everyone must be allowed to speak for an organization in his or her own way, or does it make policing the brand more important than ever? Is nonprofit strategy fundamentally distinct from for-profit strategy, or is that distinction out-of-date? To all three questions, this book answers *yes* to the initial proposition: nonprofits should invest in their brand, abandon the notion of policing their brand, and question the assumptions underlying for-profit strategy tools before applying them to their organization. Agree or not, you will quickly see that much more is at stake here than an organization's name, logo, or even communications strategy. This book goes to the very essence of what defines a nonprofit organization.

For the purposes of this brief foreword, the brand of a nonprofit might be roughly defined as the mental impression people have of the organization: the promises it makes to its clients, collaborators, or supporters and their expectations about the quality of work or the experience it provides. Those promises and expectations are evoked by the names, logos, slogans, and other communication devices used by organizations, movements, and individuals—for example, political candidates—to differentiate themselves from others. Such outward manifestations of brand are now visible in practically every inhabited place and communication vehicle on the planet.

Nonprofit organizations have typically considered their brands—if they have done so at all—as fundraising or public relations devices to help attract supporters and donors. But a nonprofit's brand is something more than an eye-catching lure. A brand is also a powerful expression of an organization's mission and values as well as a reflection of the commitment, pride, and passion its workers and collaborators have in the organization. This power makes it a matter of pride for some people to say, "I work for Doctors Without Borders," to become a member of Amnesty International, to hang a Sierra Club calendar over their desk, or to retweet an alert from Greenpeace. This power makes a nonprofit organization's brand a critical tool for clarifying its unique voice, message, and role. More, this power can help an organization engineer collaborations and partnerships that will better enable it to fulfill its mission and deepen its impact. For these reasons, the brand of a non-profit organization is a strategic asset central to the success of the organization itself.

The brands of nonprofit organizations play distinctive roles differ-ent from the brands of commercial enterprises. These differences relate to the different balance of competition and collaboration in the nonprofit and private sectors, and they relate as well to the multiplicity of value propositions, irreducible to a single monetary metric, that a nonprofit must advance with multiple audiences.

Brand management across the nonprofit sector is becoming more sophisticated, but this does not mean that it has to be expensive. Rather, it requires an organization's willingness to embrace and adopt new thinking about the development and management of a brand and to allocate time and effort to discussing its brand both internally among its workers and collaborators and externally among its outside partners and supporters. Brand communications have less to do with the outward projection of a controlled image and more to do with establishing such a dialogue: a process of participatory and authentic engagement in both the development and the communication of the organization's identity and image. Responsibility for an organization's brand should, therefore, not reside solely within its marketing, communications, or development departments; it should reside principally with an organization's execu-tive team and board. Defining and nurturing the brand should fit within the job description of every person working for an organization. And efforts to define and nurture an organization's brand should involve its supporters and benefactors as they work on the organization's behalf as advocates and ambassadors.

The brand IDEA framework presented in this book is designed to help nonprofit organizations develop and manage their brands in a way that will serve their mission while remaining true to their values and culture. The framework fits within the participatory paradigm described earlier, and it leverages opportunities made available by today's rapidly changing technological and media environment. Founded on three prin-ciples—integrity, democracy, and affinity—that produce the acronym IDEA, the framework is both a diagnostic tool for determining whether an organization is managing its brand effectively and a prescriptive model to guide organizations in their brand management efforts.

The framework can help an established organization identify possible problems with a brand. It can help an organization decide whether rebranding is needed. It can be deployed to help clarify an organization's core strategy. Examples provided in the text show how some organizations have approached and used the brand IDEA framework and how an organization operates and appears when it is managing its brand effectively.

If emerging theories and current trends of nonprofit management are any indication, these organizations will increasingly pursue their missions relying on fluid teams and networks in which access to information, assets, and responsibility will be widely shared. As this reality develops, the nonprofit brand IDEA is an essential tool for nonprofit managers.

Christopher Stone
president, Open Society Foundations

INTRODUCTION

This book is the result of more than two years of research and collaborative effort, supported by the Rockefeller Foundation, to examine the role of brand in the nonprofit sector. It is also the culmination of a decade of our own work looking into how nonprofit organizations build and manage their brands. Initially inspired by an Edelman study in 2002 which suggested that nonprofit organizations comprise the world's most trusted brands, we started on a journey to try to understand how these powerful nonprofit brands were being built and managed, and how this differed, if at all, from their commercial private sector counterparts.

In 2010, the Rockefeller Foundation recognized that brand management in the nonprofit sector and interest in nonprofit brands were at a tipping point. They also realized that nonprofit organizations often had to rely on tools designed for the private sector to manage their brands. The goal of initiating research on the role of brand in the nonprofit sector was to better understand how nonprofit organizations might more effectively use and manage their brand to achieve social impact.

We originally published our findings in an article in the Spring 2012 issue of the *Stanford Social Innovation Review* (SSIR) called "The Role of Brand in the Nonprofit Sector" (Kylander and Stone, 2012). The central organizing framework in the article and carried forward into this book is the *brand IDEA*, which stands for the related concepts of brand **I**ntegrity, brand **DE**mocracy, and brand **A**ffinity. Our initial framework also included brand Ethics as a key component of the model, but our understanding of the brand IDEA has continued to evolve, and brand Ethics has been integrated into the broader concept of brand Integrity.

Findings from the first phase of the work, consisting of in-depth interviews conducted throughout 2011 and culminating in a one-day workshop with representatives from nonprofit organizations and thought leaders, gave rise to the SSIR article. We were delighted and excited when this article was favorably received, and we spoke with a number of practitioners who found the brand IDEA framework and underlying concepts useful for the management of their brands. Inspired by this positive feedback and discussions with the publisher Jossey-Bass, we embarked on a second phase of interviews during the summer of 2012, with the intention of developing a better understanding of how the brand IDEA works in practice and of collecting detailed examples of how nonprofit organizations are effectively managing their brands using the brand IDEA to maximize their impact. Our goal was to determine how the brand IDEA framework applied both to organizations with successful brands and to those that might be wrestling with brand management issues. We also wanted to assess the extent to which the brand IDEA was useful for nonprofits with varying organizational structures and sizes and at different points in their life cycles.

During our research, we attempted to interview a spectrum of organizations, large and small, new and well established, in a variety of subsectors both within and outside the United States. Overall, during both phases of the interviews, we talked to more than one hundred men and women in nonprofit organizations, as well as to a number of academics and consultants. This book is in large part the collective reflection of their experiences, ideas, thoughts, and suggestions on how brand can enable nonprofit organizations to maximize their impact. A list of the individuals and organizations whose insights and experiences are included in this book can be found at the back of the book.

We are excited by the findings from this research, which demonstrate that brand can be a powerful asset for nonprofits. We are witnessing a paradigm shift in the way that many nonprofits think about their brand, which is reflected in the principles of the brand IDEA framework. While conducting some of our interviews, we found that the brand IDEA framework resonated deeply with those who are actively involved with nonprofit brands. In fact, we talked to several people who described how the SSIR article was critical in helping their organization accomplish their rebranding initiatives, by framing the issues of nonprofit brand management in terms that people could understand and embrace. The first online post in response to the article read, "It is great to see this focus on nonprofit branding and the framework suggested to understand the topic." Our hope is that the brand IDEA framework and the underlying concepts will inspire many other organizations to look at brand in a new way and support them in the management of their brands.

PURPOSE AND INTENT

Our purpose in writing this book is threefold:

1. To propose a new way of thinking about brand in the nonprofit sector, which we call the nonprofit paradigm shift

2. To stimulate a clearer understanding of what brand can for do for nonprofits and how it is important, which we outline in the Role of Brand Cycle

3. To provide a framework and tools to help nonprofit managers effectively manage their brands using the brand IDEA

We believe that everyone involved in nonprofit organizations, whatever his or her capacity, has a role to play in managing the brand. We hope that this book will inspire nonprofit managers, board members, funders, foundations, consultants, academics, and students and provide a new way of thinking about the critical role that brands can play in furthering mission and driving social change. The brand IDEA framework that we propose can be used both as a diagnostic tool to assess whether an organization is succeeding in its brand management efforts and as a prescriptive tool for enhancing brand management activities. We hope that through the wide variety of organizational examples offered throughout the book, you can find insight and motivation to more effectively embrace and leverage your nonprofit's brand.

We also recognize that there is still some skepticism when talking about brands in the nonprofit sector. Indeed, there is a sometimes a visceral reaction to the very word *brand*, which some of our interviewees refer to as the "B word." Sometimes people working in the nonprofit sector dismiss the notion of brand as a somewhat irrelevant for-profit concept. This, we believe, is largely because of the perception of brand as a fundraising and PR tool. This skepticism, though understandable, may be limiting the ability of these organizations to implement their missions effectively. At the same time, a greater number of brand proponents and enthusiasts, often with backgrounds in the private sector, are starting to actively manage nonprofit brands. However, they may be using models and approaches from the private sector that are not always well adapted. Our intent is therefore to help bridge this divide between brand proponents and skeptics by encouraging a new brand management mindset and by providing the brand IDEA framework, which uses concepts and terminology that can engage all stakeholders and that are adapted and specific to the nonprofit sector.

This book also addresses a need for guidelines and tools to assist nonprofits in the management of their brands, and discusses brand in terms that are relevant and familiar to those working with nonprofits: mission, values, engagement, and partnerships. Although the concepts may not necessarily be easy to implement, they are not complex. This book can be useful both to those with a background in marketing and branding and to those who do not have any prior experience or knowledge in this field. Board members who want to understand the concepts of brand management for nonprofits will have a new and, we hope, more helpful way of thinking about brand. Nonprofit managers at all levels will understand how their work, whatever the function, ultimately contributes to and supports the brand. Nonprofit leaders and consultants will have a tool for diagnosing brand management and guiding rebranding efforts. Finally, academics and students will have background information that draws from a number of academic sources to expand their understanding of nonprofit brand. The many quotations and examples throughout the text help bring the brand IDEA and brand management theory to life for all audiences.

Nonprofits and their brands are growing in importance and stature. Nonprofit organizations command tremendous levels of trust with the public, and their brand valuations are on par with those of major corporations. According to the 2012 Edelman trust barometer report, nonprofits, for the fifth year in a row, remain the most trusted institutions globally. Over the last decade there has been increasing interest in nonprofit brands and branding. As Aaron Hurst, founder and CEO of Taproot Foundation, a national nonprofit consulting group, explained, "There has been a tremendous increase in this topic in the ten years since I started the Taproot Foundation. In 2002, it was hard to get a nonprofit leader to see the value of brand, but it has since become the most requested area of support from the Taproot Foundation." Our work is intended to help all nonprofit organizations, large and small, build stronger brands, thereby increasing trust and organizational cohesion, capacity, and impact.

SUMMARY OF CONTENTS

This book is organized into three parts. Part One, "Context, Concepts, and Building Blocks," outlines the context, concepts and definitions, and building blocks of brand, setting the stage for the brand IDEA framework itself. Chapter One provides an overview of the broader context shaping the nonprofit sector today and the paradigm shift that we believe is driving a change in the way brand is perceived and managed by nonprofit organizations. This chapter also discusses two trends that are changing the environment for nonprofits: the rise in social media and networking, and the increase in partnerships and collaborative action. We also provide an overview of the brand IDEA framework and discuss how this framework is aligned with many of the exciting new ideas and theories of nonprofit management. For audiences for whom brand management is a new concept, Chapter Two includes definitions of brand and brand management, and a discussion of how nonprofit brand management differs from that of private sector organizations. Some background information on brand equity and its drivers is also included. Chapter Three reviews the building blocks of brand, the principles of differentiation and positioning, and the concept of theory of change. This chapter also includes a discussion of internal branding, which we believe plays an important role in nonprofit brand management. Our research identified a number of sources of skepticism toward brand and branding within the nonprofit sector, and we address these in Chapter Four. This chapter also revisits the brand paradigm shift outlined in the first chapter and articulates the benefits of brand management for nonprofits in terms of the Role of Brand Cycle. The Role of Brand Cycle illustrates the positive outcomes that a strong brand can have in terms of building trust and organizational cohesion, and supporting capacity and impact.

Part Two, Getting the Brand IDEA, defines each of the brand IDEA principles in detail. Chapters Five, Six, and Seven describe brand Integrity, brand Democracy, and brand Affinity, respectively. In each chapter, we break down the concept and bring each to life with examples and experiences from our research. Throughout these chapters, we offer detailed examples of how a number of nonprofit organizations are following a brand IDEA approach, or "living the brand IDEA." We also identify potential challenges in each of these areas.

Part Three, Putting the Brand IDEA into Action, offers practical advice on implementing the brand IDEA framework. Chapter Eight suggests how to implement brand Integrity through brand Democracy and how to create brand Affinity for impact, with specific recommendations, guidelines, and tools. This chapter also suggests an approach for measuring the impact or return on investment of implementing the brand IDEA by monitoring organizational cohesion and trust. Chapter Nine addresses brand management in specific situations, for different organizational structures, and at varying stages of the organizational life cycle. Finally, a brief conclusion highlights the characteristics of an organization that fully embraces the brand IDEA framework, and summarizes the roles and actions that individuals can take to support brand initiatives in the organizations they care about.

HOW TO USE THIS BOOK

For those looking for some background and context on what a brand is, how for-profit and nonprofit brand management differ, the role of brand in nonprofits, and an overview of the brand IDEA framework, Part One will be most helpful. If you want to gain a deeper understanding of brand Identity, brand Democracy, and brand Affinity and wish to explore the details of these concepts through concrete examples, you may want to start with Chapter One and then delve directly into Part Two. Finally, if you want to use the brand IDEA framework as a diagnostic or prescriptive tool, you may choose to focus more on Part Three, where you will find detailed implementation guidelines for each part of the framework.

PART

1

CONTEXT, CONCEPTS, AND BUILDING BLOCKS

CHAPTER

1

WHAT IS DRIVING THE PARADIGM SHIFT AND BRAND IDEA FRAMEWORK

We believe that current trends are making brand management increasingly important for nonprofit organizations and that brand management must be understood as part of a new paradigm. This chapter describes the background and context for our research, including current forces that we believe are affecting nonprofits. We also discuss the paradigm shift we uncovered during the most recent phase in our research into how brands are being perceived and managed. The chapter includes an introduction to the brand IDEA framework and an overview of how this framework is consistent with the zeitgeist of current management thinking.

BACKGROUND AND CONTEXT

The world of nonprofit leaders and managers has changed substantially over the past decade. The number of nonprofits has skyrocketed (according to the Urban Institute, between 2001 and 2011, the number of nonprofits in the United States alone increased 25 percent—from 1,259,764 million to 1,574,674 million), and competition for funding has intensified. Global economic factors have dampened availability of funding, and at the same time, environmental, social, economic, and humanitarian needs have increased. New forms of nonprofit organizations, such as social enterprises, have emerged, and new technological and communication capabilities have revolutionized the way nonprofits interact with their publics. The boundaries between traditional sectors are increasingly blurred, and some people believe that a fourth sector (for-benefit hybrids) is emerging (Sabeti, 2011). Partnerships and alliances of all types, both within and across sectors, have proliferated and created new options and challenges for nonprofit organizations. We are seeing more networked coalitions and alliances that bring together multiple autonomous organizations, often from different sectors, to address complex social issues.

We believe that two major trends are of particular relevance to nonprofit brands today: changes in communications technology, including the rise in social media and networking, and the increase in partnerships and collaborative action. The impact of these two key trends on nonprofit brands and how they relate to the brand IDEA framework are captured in Figure 1.1. Let's turn to a brief discussion of these two forces and how they influence brand management in the nonprofit sector.

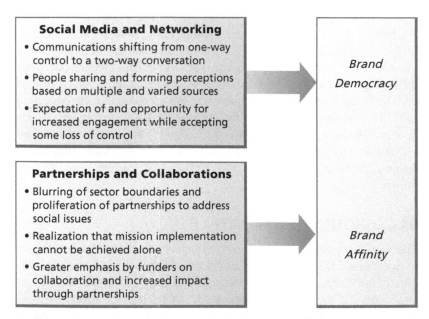

FIGURE 1.1.   *Key Trends Impacting Nonprofit Brands*

Social Media and Networking

Social media and social networking sites, blogs, and other forms of virtual communities have fundamentally changed the way a nonprofit interacts with its stakeholders and brand audiences. Social media has the potential to reach large numbers of people quickly and at a low cost, but is difficult, if not impossible, to control. As Sherine Jayawickrama (2011), domain manager at the Hauser Institute for Civil Society at Harvard University, notes in her report on NGOs and social media, "Social media is a collaborative space where ideas are open sourced and the wisdom of the crowd is valued. [It] offers a platform for two-way conversations that can only be optimized if organizations are open to feedback, listen well and respond quickly" (p. 1). She describes the changes that have resulted as "traditional communications and public relations cultures of INGOs [International Nongovernmental Organizations] have had to adapt—generating compelling content quickly, speeding up approvals processes and engaging with comments and questions of all sorts—as they move from a broadcast model to a conversation model" (p. 1). She concludes that "effective social networks require some degree of self-organization which requires [nonprofits] to step back and not seek control of conversations focused on them" (p. 1).

In essence, social media has shifted communications from a one-way control of information to a number of dialogues, some of which may not even include the organization (for example, among supporters). Social media and networking have also shifted expectations for engagement and participation: participants actively share thoughts, photos, stories, and advice. People are forming images and perceptions of organizations based on what they experience, see, hear, and read. Other potential partner organizations are likewise forming perceptions about whether or not to work with each other, based on all available information, some of which comes from sources outside the organization.

Dixon and Keyes (2013) suggest that social media has "changed the ways in which people can influence others and increased the range of meaningful calls to action available to nonprofits" (p. 29). They add that "continuous communication is now an expectation." Although the changes wrought by social media and the demands those changes bring might seem overwhelming, we think that social media also presents nonprofit organizations with fantastic opportunities and has few barriers to entry. Supporters can be embraced and encouraged to participate in a myriad of activities that go beyond simple financial donations, and internal and external "ambassadors" can be tapped to widely communicate and drive support for the organization. The loss of control this entails concerns some organizations, but Dixon and Keyes believe that the cost-benefit ratio is still positive, particularly because "with the loss of some control comes an increase in authenticity and transparency" (p. 29). We believe that nonprofits must embrace the reality that social media has changed the way people engage with and talk about their organizations. Strict control and policing of their brands is no longer useful or possible. This loss of control and change in expectations are at the heart of brand Democracy and are one of the drivers of our new approach to brand management.

Partnerships and Collaborations

Partnerships between organizations of all kinds have proliferated over the past decade, and the division or boundaries between the three traditional sectors (nonprofit, for-profit, and government) are blurring, both as a cause and as a result of this increase. Yankey and Willen (2010) believe that this increase in partnerships is being driven by two main factors: the growing realization that many nonprofits cannot achieve their social missions alone, and the economic climate and shifts in funding and funding requirements. Institutional funders in particular are increasingly requiring a demonstration of effectiveness and collaborative approaches.

Austin (2000) defines cross-sector partnerships along a continuum, with philanthropic relationships at one end (essentially corporate donations to nonprofits), a transaction stage (with a focus on specific activities), and an integrative stage resulting in joint ventures. Pohle and Hittner (2008) take this framework one step further by including the collaboration between multiple companies and multiple nonprofits. These authors describe the issues undertaken by these collaborations or networks as "meta-problems" that are complex and that require a long-term commitment by all parties. Indeed, the nonprofit landscape is marked by the increasing convergence of multi-stakeholder collaborations and complex coalitions (between nonprofits, business, governmental entities, and multilateral institutions), which aim to collectively affect a wide range of social issues. As the boundaries between the actors from different sectors and the goals they pursue become increasingly blurred, nonprofits must adapt to this changing landscape and to the increasing role that businesses and, to a lesser extent, governments are playing. If nothing else, nonprofits have a critical role to play in shaping the way that these players effect social change (Bulloch, 2009). For-profit entities are increasingly entering what was once traditional nonprofit territory, and nonprofit organizations must decide how they want to react. They could resist this "encroachment," or they could actively engage these for-profit players and shape the way these entities work and their joint outcomes. This partnership and collaborative imperative is another factor that argues for a new approach to brand management. It underlies the concept of brand Affinity, whereby non-profit organizations use and leverage their brands, not only on behalf of their own organizations but also to drive shared social impact.

A PARADIGM SHIFT AND BRAND MANAGEMENT MINDSET

In line with the changes around social media and partnerships we've discussed, our research and discussions uncovered an essential paradigm shift that is starting to occur in the nonprofit sector. This shift involves a change in the perception of the role of the brand, away from a fundraising and PR tool to a critical strategic asset focused on mission implementation. Instead of thinking of the brand as a logo and tagline, the new paradigm understands brand as the embodiment of the organization's mission and values. This expanded definition of brand was described by many of our interviewees. Joan Barlow, creative services manager at the Robert Wood Johnson Foundation, for example, recognized that "brand is more than colors, design, and a logo." She described the new understanding of brand as "the pride we feel in our work, our culture of commitment and passion, and our values."

Rather than focusing on fundraising as the objective of the brand, the new paradigm places brand in service of the mission and social impact. Instead of having responsibility for the brand reside within the marketing, communications, or development department, responsibility for the brand as a key strategic asset resides with the entire executive team and the board, although as we will argue later, brand management is everyone's job.

In the new brand paradigm, brand has less to do with gaining a competitive advantage and more to do with clarifying positioning, which can help in determining the collaborations and partnerships that enable an organization to implement its mission and maximize its impact. Brand communications have less to do with the one-way projecting of a controlled image and more to do with establishing a dialogue and a process of participative and authentic engagement, in both the development and the communication of the brand. The brand audience used to be thought of as the donors (both individual and institutional), but in the new paradigm, the brand must address a whole spectrum of both internal and external audiences that are ready and willing to support the organization in different ways as brand ambassadors. We find this shift very exciting and believe that it can truly catalyze nonprofit organizations to implement their missions more effectively and efficiently.

Some people tell us, "We are a small organization with limited resources, and we don't have the time or money to do branding." Others say, "I think it would be a good idea for us to manage our brand more effectively, but I wouldn't even know where to start." Our response to both of these concerns is that brand management does not necessarily require a significant financial investment or specific expertise. What it does require is a willingness to adopt a new brand management mindset and allocate the time, effort, and energy to widely discussing brand internally. As Ingrid Srinath, executive director of Childline India, said, "You have a brand whether you like it or not. Really the only choice you have is how actively you want to shape and manage that brand." Embracing this new nonprofit brand paradigm is the first step for organizations that want to actively shape and manage their brands. Table 1.1 summarizes the key elements of this paradigm shift.

We believe that organizations need to leverage the opportunities that are emerging with the rise in social media and the increased emphasis on partnerships. The brand IDEA framework, to which we now turn, is intended to help organizations leverage these recent trends and integrate

TABLE 1.1. *The Nonprofit Brand Paradigm Shift*

Brand Element	Old Paradigm	New Paradigm
Definition	A logo	Strategic asset that embodies the mission and values
Goal	Fundraising and PR	Mission impact
Positioning	Competitive advantage	Clarity and effective partnerships
Communications	One-way projection of a specific image	Participative engagement
Audiences	Donors	Internal and external stakeholders
Organizational home	Marketing and communications	Executive team, board, and all brand ambassadors
Requirements	Money and expertise	A brand management mindset

the elements of the new paradigm. The framework allows organizations to manage their brands in a way that recognizes the strategic nature and mission impact of a brand, encourages participative engagement with internal and external stakeholders, and addresses the important role the brand plays in promoting partnerships.

INTRODUCTION TO THE BRAND IDEA

The brand IDEA encompasses three principles: brand Integrity, brand Democracy, and brand Affinity. A brief description of these three principles and the outcomes they produce are summarized in Table 1.2. As we will see in Chapter Five, brand Integrity places the mission and values at the center of the brand and is the result of the alignment between mission, values, and brand identity on the one hand and brand identity and image on the other. To be clear, the word *integrity* here

TABLE 1.2. *Principles of the Brand IDEA Framework*

Principle	Description	Outcome
Brand Integrity	• Structural alignment between brand identity and mission, strategy, and values • Structural alignment between internal brand identity and external brand image	• Results in organizational cohesion and trust
Brand Democracy	• Participative process of internal and external stakeholder engagement to both define and communicate the brand	• Creates brand ambassadors and reduces the need for control
Brand Affinity	• Approach that leverages brand in support of partnerships and collaboration • Use of the brand and brand assets to focus on shared social objectives	• Drives greater mission implementation and social impact

is used in the sense of structural integrity or alignment, and not just moral integrity. When the organization's values and mission are consistently aligned with its brand identity, and when this identity is consistently aligned with the external image, the nonprofit brand is able to establish a clear, distinct, consistent, and credible position in the minds of both internal and external stakeholders. Internally, a brand with high structural integrity connects the mission to the identity of the organization, giving board members, staff, volunteers, and other internal stakeholders a common sense of who the organization is, what it does, and why it matters in the world. Externally, a brand with high structural integrity firmly aligns brand identity and brand image, so that there is no disconnect between the internal and external perceptions of the brand. When the brand image truly reflects the brand identity and the brand identity reflects the mission, the brand is authentic, consistent, and powerfully positioned to create organizational cohesion and trust among all the organization's stakeholders.

Having a clear brand identity gives one the ability to succinctly describe who the organization is, what it stands for, and why it is important. It's about knowing how and why your organization is making a difference and how it differs from other players, and letting that knowledge guide your decisions and actions. "Isn't that just my mission?" we have been asked. In a way, it is. Both the organization's mission and its values should be embedded in the brand identity. However, we believe that it is also how that brand identity is developed and communicated, as well as how the brand is managed to maximize mission impact, that are important in the brand IDEA framework.

Brand image comprises the feelings and perceptions that exist in the hearts and minds of external stakeholders when they think about your organization. The alignment between who you are (identity) and how people perceive you (image) is what creates powerful, trusted brands and is at the heart of the brand Integrity principle.

Part of brand Integrity is also concerned with ensuring that the brand itself and the way in which the brand is deployed embody and reflect the core values of the organization. Just as brand Integrity aligns and cements the brand with mission, it also aligns both the brand identity and the brand image with the core values and culture of the organization. Not only is the establishment of a brand rooted in ethics and values; the *use* of that brand, internally and externally, is also anchored in those same ethics and values.

Alignment doesn't depend on large budgets and slick advertising. The ability to create brand Integrity lies in brand Democracy, a participative process that engages people throughout the organization and beyond the organization's boundaries, with the result that all stakeholders become brand ambassadors. Brand Integrity can be thought of as a desired state or goal; brand Democracy, to which we now turn, is, in part, the means or process by which brand Integrity is achieved.

As we will discuss in more detail in Chapter Six, brand Democracy is the process of engaging internal and external stakeholders. It means that the nonprofit organization trusts its members, staff, participants, and volunteers to participate in both the development of the organization's brand identity and the communication of that identity. By brand Democracy, we do not mean that everyone gets to "vote" on the brand, but it does mean that there is stakeholder participation. Internal and external stakeholders are engaged in the process of defining, refining, articulating, and communicating the organization's brand identity. In this way, everyone develops a clear understanding of the organization's core identity and can become an effective brand advocate and ambassador. Every employee and volunteer authentically and personally communicates the essence of the brand. As a result, the need to exert control over how the brand is presented and portrayed in order to ensure strict consistency is largely eliminated. Noah Manduke, former president of social sector brand consultancy Durable Good and chief strategy officer, Jeff Skoll Group, conveyed the essence of brand Democracy, explaining that organizations need "a deliberate process that brings people from awareness (I know) to understanding (I know why) to adoption (I know how) to internalizing the brand (I believe)."

With the rise in social media, brand control is becoming increasingly difficult, if not impossible. We believe that the concept of brand Democracy extends beyond the traditional boundaries of the organization, which are becoming increasingly porous, to include external audiences, such as patrons, donors, volunteers, partners, supporters, or anyone blogging or tweeting about an organization. Brand Democracy does not imply brand anarchy. What it does suggest is a new approach to brand management that promotes the participative engagement of all stakeholders in both the definition and communication of the brand. When brand Democracy is conducted with a view to achieving brand Integrity, the organization's mission and values define the context for brand Democracy and provide the parameters or bounds guiding its implementation. The process of brand Democracy itself engages stakeholders in a meaningful way, creating organizational cohesion and consistency in internal understanding and adoption of brand identity. Brand Democracy taps into the opportunities that social media creates and engages external audiences, enabling organizations to more effectively implement their mission and drive social impact.

Brand Affinity is an approach to brand management whose focus is on shared social impact, rather than on individual organizational goals. Increasingly, many nonprofit organizations recognize that their ambitious, multifaceted, and long-term social objectives cannot be achieved alone, and that they need partners if they are to achieve the impact they seek. Organizations implementing brand Affinity use their brands in support of these broad social goals, in a way that goes beyond capacity building for their own individual organizations. Brands with high brand Affinity work well with other organizations and their brands, sharing space and credit generously, promoting collective over individual interests, and emphasizing the external goal and cause rather than the individual organization.

Brand Affinity is a brand management approach designed to address complex issues that require the participation of multiple organizations. It is especially important for coalition and movement brands, for which a unique brand identity and image can be created to support a common cause. Brand Affinity taps into the power of partnerships, using brands collaboratively to drive mission and maximize social impact.

BEING IN THE ZEITGEIST

Many of the themes outlined in our description of the paradigm shift and the brand IDEA framework are ones that are also emerging in discussions of theories relevant to nonprofit management. These themes (boundaryless organizations, organizational transparency, decentralization, mission focus, collective action, collaboration, and trust) come from a variety of sources and contexts, yet they imply the same type of organizational shifts as the brand IDEA. This section discusses a number of these emerging social change ideas and management theories and connects them with specific aspects of the brand IDEA framework. This is by no means an exhaustive review, yet it demonstrates how the brand IDEA framework fits within a broader context of current social and managerial changes.

Organizational Porosity

Organizational porosity can be defined as the extent to which resources, people, information, activities, and skills flow across traditional organizational boundaries. The concept of the boundaryless organization is not new, and it suggests that the removal of boundaries both internally and between an organization and its key external constituents can result in greater flexibility and efficiency (Hirschhorn and Gilmore, 1992). Porous organizations are composed of people and groups that have common goals and shared interests but are not bound to each other by hierarchical or financial relationships. Membership in these new organizations is fluid, and participants come and go, their roles, activities, and interests evolving over time.

This new kind of organization has been described as an open or porous network, one in which the boundaries are highly permeable across functional interest areas within the organization, as well as between the organization and the external environment (Bartone and Wells, 2009). Martin (2012) suggests that we will increasingly see organizations whose strategic choices extend to networked stakeholders, partners, suppliers, and even competitors. This increase in organizational boundary porosity is due in part to the growth in open sourcing and flexible work arrangements.

The recognition that an organization's boundaries are porous can be very liberating. It can help organizations understand that key resources and partnerships might reside outside the traditional organization and that these resources can be leveraged and mobilized to achieve specific external social goals. Our concepts of brand Democracy and brand Affinity draw directly on this notion of organizational porosity. Focusing on common interests, creating relationships with external stakeholders that are more democratic and allow for give and take, and becoming more open in terms of sharing brand assets, materials, and information all build on this concept of organizational porosity.

Open Innovation

At a recent meeting that looked at how to globalize models for social change, open innovation communities were identified as a way to accelerate social impact (Clay and Paul, 2012). Clay and Paul suggest that "open innovation communities are characterized by transparent communication, decentralized decision making, and widely distributed action" (p. 17). Using an open-source approach to scaling social change means involving external stakeholders (such as beneficiaries) in decision making and problem solving, and connecting with people inside and outside the organization. "Traditional beneficiaries become innovators in their own right, able to evolve, iterate and shape a given product or service" (p. 17). This is a similar approach to that of brand Democracy, which engages both internal and external stakeholders in the development and communication of the brand. Clay and Paul also suggest moving toward an ecosystem perspective, creating open-source tools from your own enterprise for use by others. "No longer exclusively concerned with the individual interests of your own organization, you naturally start empowering other actors and organizations that share your vision and commitment by offering your tools and services" (p. 18). This is akin to the concept of brand Affinity, whereby brand assets are used to promote partnerships and collaborations that further shared social objectives.

Collective Impact

Kania and Kramer (2011) articulate a theory of collective impact, describing an approach that closely parallels our concept of brand Affinity. They suggest that abandoning individual agendas in favor of a collective approach achieves a much greater impact. "Large-scale social change comes from better cross-sector coordination rather than from the isolated intervention of individual organizations" (p. 36). They indicate that "examples of collective impact are addressing social issues that, like education, require many different players to change their behavior in order to solve a complex problem" (p. 38). Creating a movement for change is an important aspect of this theory. "Unlike most collaborations, collective impact initiatives involve a centralized infrastructure, a dedicated staff, and a structured process that leads to a common agenda, shared measurement, continuous communication, and mutually reinforcing activities among all participants" (p. 38). In a follow-up article (Hanleybrown, Kania, and Kramer, 2012), the authors touch on the "softer dimensions of a successful change effort, such as relationship and trust building among diverse stakeholders." As we shall see, brand plays an important role in building trust, and brand Affinity espouses the use of the brand to promote collective goals over individual goals.

During a roundtable discussion on collective impact moderated by Eric Nee and Michele Jolin (2012), Hecht tied the notion of organizational self-reflection with that of collective impact. "Self reflection has been hugely missing from most organizations," he summarized. "One of the reasons that collective impact is picking up is that more people are reflecting" (p. 28). Our belief is that using a brand Democracy approach to building brand Integrity is one way in which organizations can really reflect on their mission and desired impact relative to other players in the ecosystem, and is an important precursor to being able to implement brand Affinity and achieve collective impact.

Corporate Social Responsibility and Shared Value

The concept of corporate social responsibility (CSR) emerged in the 1970s and has now been widely adopted by the private sector, particularly large international corporations and new enterprises. It is generally perceived as beneficial for the long-term success of for-profit organizations, and is expressed as the notion of "doing well by doing good." Sprinkle and Maines (2010) refer to CSR as the "range of corporate activities that focus on the welfare of stakeholder groups other than investors" (p. 446). In many of these endeavors, corporations partner with nonprofit organizations so as to achieve and implement their CSR initiatives (Peloza and Falkenberg, 2009). A recent study by IBM of 250 large companies found that although companies tend to talk about CSR in terms of philanthropy, many companies also perceive CSR as a plat-form for opportunity and growth (Pohle and Hittner, 2008). Pohle and Hittner suggest that increasingly, companies are (1) thinking about CSR as an investment rather than a cost, (2) talking about CSR in terms of transparency rather than visibility, and (3) moving their relationships (particularly with nonprofits) from containment to engagement. We believe that this evolution of CSR is positive for the nonprofit sector as a whole and sets the stage for increasingly effective cross-sector partnerships.

Porter and Kramer (2011) have developed and argued for the notion of shared value, "which involves creating economic value in a way that also creates value for society by addressing its needs and challenges" (p. 65). They believe that for-profits and businesses must reconnect company success with social progress and that "shared value is not social responsibility, philanthropy, or even sustainability, but a new way to achieve economic success" (p. 65). These authors add that shared value "is not on the margin of what companies do, but at the center," and believe that "it can give rise to the next major transformation of business thinking based on a far deeper appreciation of societal needs, a greater understanding of the true bases of company productivity, and the ability to collaborate across profit/nonprofit boundaries" (p. 65). This widely embraced notion of shared value will continue to drive opportunities for collaboration between the nonprofit and private sectors and strongly supports our brand Affinity approach.

Leadership

Current thinking about personal leadership parallels many of the con-cepts in the brand IDEA framework. During the roundtable on collective impact (Nee and Jolin, 2012), Schmitz discussed the role of nonprofit leaders: "We train nonprofit leaders to be great fundraisers . . . [Collec-tive impact] is about engaging communities and being vulnerable. It's not about self-promotion of your organization or of you. It actually goes against a lot of the activities that people get rewarded for traditionally. We need to train our leaders to be more collaborative, to be more inclu-sive, and to have greater integrity. It's a whole different set of practices"

(p. 29). In his book *Everyone Leads*, Schmitz (2011) talks about an active process of leadership that engages others. This collaborative form of leadership focuses on shared values and common goals, echoing key aspects of both brand Democracy and brand Integrity.

Stephen Parker, a leadership and organizational change expert, suggests that "the ability to inspire others stems more from who you are as a person than from what you say or do. Achieving clarity about your core convictions and values is critical. Knowing and being comfortable with who you are sits at the heart of your ability to be authentic, while your ability to share your values and beliefs creates resonance and builds deep trust with your followers." In a similar way, we believe that organizations that have a clear understanding of who they are, and whose brand identity is firmly rooted in their values and mission, can achieve brand Integrity and are in a good position to build strong brand equity, elicit trust, and exert leadership and influence to drive change through brand Affinity.

Exponential Fundraising

Jennifer McCrea's work on exponential fundraising also aligns well with the concepts of the brand IDEA. McCrea, senior research fellow at the Hauser Institute for Civil Society at Harvard University, argues in favor of relationship building over traditional fundraising. She also holds workshops that include learning how to identify partners who share a collaborative worldview (and can make your organization stronger, not drain its resources) and how to deepen core relationships for exponential results.

> Too often, fundraising is seen strictly as a way of raising money. It is transactional and based on a consumer model designed around a buyer (the donor) and a seller (the organization). As a result, relationships are money-centered and asymmetrical, built on expectations, needs and external circumstances, not on mutual accountability, collaboration and internal growth. The buyer/seller dynamic leaves philanthropists feeling controlled and discouraged by the lack of genuine partnership and organizations feeling over-dependent and frustrated by perceived donor meddling.
>
> Exponential Fundraising re-conceptualizes fundraising as something that is not only mission critical, but a vehicle to fundamentally transform organizations and the people who are involved with them.

Partnerships are designed from the start to be co-creative and generative—and strategy is built on a growing and continuous resource flow that is designed to break down walls, not create them. (2013)

Fundraising is moving toward a focus on partnerships that are based on a mission and created around a cause and that employ open, collaborative approaches. Fundraising becomes the job of everyone in the organization, with a focus on building relationships and being authentic. This relates closely to our notion of empowering brand ambassadors throughout and even beyond the organization through brand Democracy.

McCrea also notes that "people aren't parrots. Squawking an agreed upon organizational line doesn't move the agenda or others forward." She advocates for "letting your partners discover what to say based on their own experience and their own reasons for being a part of the work you are doing together. When it comes from the inside out, not the other way around, it is not only more authentic, it sticks. Don't be afraid to let go of some control," she urges. "It's the only way you're really going to grow" (2012). This focus on collaboration and trust and on letting go of brand control strongly parallels brand Democracy. On her blog, McCrea discusses how shared values can motivate action, and notes that exponential growth occurs through collaboration, "Real, enduring strength lies much more in partnerships, in community and interdependence, than it does in trying to go it alone" (2010). This approach is also clearly in line with our notion of brand Affinity.

Nonprofit Networking

Much has been written about the importance to nonprofits of developing networks. Networks can be seen as one approach to achieving brand Affinity. Wei-Skillern and Marciano (2008) suggest that nonprofit networks are essential to achieving greater mission impact. "Nonprofit leaders should put the pursuit of their missions—not the growth of their organizations—back at the center of all of their organizations' activities. They should identify their organizations' unique competencies and actively seek partnerships with other organizations that will help them serve their missions more efficiently and effectively. They should look to both complementary and competing organizations as potential partners" (p. 43). Brand Affinity, including the use of brand to select and support partnerships, is entirely consistent with this view.

Wei-Skillern and Marciano (2008) also underscore the importance of shared values, which can help generate trust and reduce the need for strict controls, and describe partnerships in terms that move beyond organizational boundaries. "Networked nonprofits forge long-term partnerships with trusted peers to tackle their missions on multiple fronts. And unlike traditional nonprofit leaders who think of their organizations as hubs and their partners as spokes, networked nonprofit leaders think of their organizations as nodes within a broad constellation that revolves around shared missions and values" (p. 40).

Kanter (2012) suggests that nonprofit organizations that are more open and participatory are also more effective. This concept relates closely to our notion of brand Democracy, suggesting that nonprofits more holistically involve stakeholders. Kanter notes that "a network mindset exercises leadership through active participation, openness, decentralized decision-making, and collective action. It means operating with an awareness of the networks the organization is embedded in, and listening to and cultivating these networks to achieve impact. It means sharing by default and communicating through a network model, rather than a broadcast model—finding where the conversations are happening and taking part."

Kanter focuses largely on what organizations can be doing with social media at different stages. "[The framework] Crawl, Walk, Run, Fly . . . is designed to help [nonprofit organizations] understand and measure the nature of the change process as they move through it." Integrating this participatory engagement strategy across the organization is similar to the approach of listening to and engaging with both internal and external stakeholders inherent in brand Democracy.

Shifts in Monitoring and Evaluation

Logistic frameworks or results-based management systems are among the foremost monitoring and evaluation (M&E) systems being used in the nonprofit sector. These M&E systems have largely become the standard (Rugh, 2008), but the M&E landscape is becoming more nuanced. Many donors and nonprofits are questioning the extent to which they can ever attribute broad social changes to their own funding dollars or programs. For example, the International Development Research Council underscores the importance of contribution (as opposed to attribution) frameworks and has developed the use of outcome mapping, which outlines the importance of multiple stakeholders' contributions in effecting social change. This shift from attribution to contribution in the M&E space allows for more collaborative approaches and a focus on shared external social goals, which is at the heart of our brand Affinity.

Donors, such as the Ford Foundation, are also calling for more nuance and greater M&E attention to donors' contributions to longer-term changes (Klugman, 2009). Klugman suggests that donors should be focusing on developing theories of change that account for how they expect changes to be produced through their grant dollars, limiting their analysis, particularly in terms of advocacy, to their contribution to changes in organizational capacity, base of support, alliances, data and analysis from a social justice perspective, and policies. These trends in M&E systems strongly support the brand IDEA.

These exciting trends and emerging models paint a compelling picture of the future environment for nonprofit organizations. Although they by no means represent a complete analysis, they do provide a broader context that persuasively supports the brand IDEA framework.

SUMMARY

The world of nonprofits is characterized by an increasing number of players, fewer funding opportunities, and increasing social needs. Two trends are of particular importance to nonprofit brands: changes in communication technology (including social media) and the increase in partnerships and collaborations. We also have observed the emergence of a paradigm shift in the way nonprofit actors perceive and understand brand. This shift has led to a view of brand not as a fundraising tool but as a critical strategic asset, one that embodies the organization's mission and values and supports broad participative engagement and collaborations that maximize impact.

The brand IDEA framework sits within this new paradigm and encompasses three principles: brand Integrity, brand Democracy, and brand Affinity. Brand Integrity suggests that the mission and values of an organization be aligned with its brand identity and that this brand identity be aligned with its brand image. Brand Democracy is a process that engages both internal and external stakeholders in the development, articulation, and communication of the brand identity. Brand Affinity is the use of the brand in support of external goals achieved through partnerships and collaboration.

The brand IDEA framework resonates strongly with a number of current and emerging social change and management theories. These include organizational porosity, open innovation, collective impact, CSR and shared value, current thinking on leadership, exponential fundraising, nonprofit networking, and shifts in monitoring and evaluation.

Having established the context and drivers behind the brand IDEA framework, we turn in the next chapter to an in-depth discussion of the definitions of brand and brand management.

CHAPTER

2

WHAT IS A BRAND ANYWAY, AND WHY SHOULD YOU MANAGE IT?

Although it is easy to identify well-known brands, it is difficult to accurately describe what a brand actually is and what it does. In this chapter, we attempt to break this question down and start looking at how to manage brands. Because the majority of brand literature and brand management models emanate from the private sector, we will review these and discuss how the differences between the sectors offer us some insights into brand management for nonprofits. Finally, we discuss what makes a strong brand and how the drivers of brand equity may be somewhat different for nonprofit brands.

WHAT *IS* A BRAND?

Brand as a concept is quite elusive and can be difficult to define. We start many of our graduate classes with this very question, and students struggle to come up with definitions and these differ. A brief review of the literature on brands in the for-profit sector can help shed some light on this deceptively simple question. Kotler (2000) defines a brand as "a name, term, symbol or design, or a combination of them, which is intended to signify the goods or services of one seller or group of sellers and to differentiate them from those of competitors" (p. 36). Aaker (1991), among others, asserts that a company's brand is one of the most important intangible assets it possesses. Bedbury and Fenichell (2002) describe a brand as "a psychological concept, held in the minds of the public" (p. 15). Lencastre and Corte-Real (2010) have integrated these definitions into a construct with three components: "the identity sign itself; the marketing object to which the sign refers; and the market response to the sign" (p. 400).

Everything and everyone has a brand. Brands are associated both with tangible entities, such as products, companies, places, organizations, and people, and with intangibles, such as services, ideas, and experiences. A brand helps customers and brand audiences identify and differentiate between options, as well as develop trust. In fact, Morrison and Firmstone (2000) believe that "brands function in the same way as trust, by simplifying decision making and acting as summarized knowledge" (p. 607).

The way a brand is defined in the nonprofit literature is largely the same. Daw and Cone (2011) argue that a nonprofit brand is "a collection of perceptions about an organization, formed by every communication, action and interaction" (p. 20); Cuesta (2003) adds that a nonprofit brand is "the shared emotional perception participants and supporters hold in connection with the programs and services a nonprofit offers" (p. 1). For Sargeant (2009), nonprofit brands "are in essence a promise to the public that an organization possesses certain features or will behave in certain ways" (p. 157). According to Andreasen and Kotler (2007), nonprofit brands "imply certain information, convey certain emotions, and can even have their own personality" (p. 173).

When we asked our interviewees to define brand in the nonprofit sector, many of them used similar definitions and language. Some described brand as an "intangible asset" or as "a promise." Others felt that a brand captures the persona of an organization by representing its very "soul or essence." Yet others identified the brand in terms of both what is projected and what is perceived. Finally, brand was seen as a source of efficiency, "a shortcut" allowing potential donors, clients, and partners to save time in decision making.

The definitions of what a brand actually *is* in the nonprofit sector are not fundamentally different from the for-profit definitions outlined earlier. Brand in both sectors can be defined as an intangible asset and identifier that imparts information and creates perceptions and emotions in its audiences. What also emerges from both the literature and our interviews is that we can break brand down into two dimensions: the brand identity, which is an internal reflection (representing personality, soul, and essence) and an asset; and the brand image, which is the external perception that creates connection with audiences. It is also important to note that although brands can be associated with programs, products, or services in both the nonprofit and for-profit sectors, the definitions here and our focus in this book describe the organizational brand.

We have found that some people equate *brand* with *organization*, using the word "brand" when they are referring to an organizational entity. Although a brand represents an organization, it is not itself an organizational entity. Brand is also sometimes confused with reputation. The two concepts are certainly related, but are different. Reputation has been defined as the "collective representation of multiple constituencies' image of a company built over time based on a company's performance and how constituencies perceive its behavior" (Argenti and Druckenmiller, 2004, p. 369). In our opinion, reputation is the sum of external perceptions or images of a brand across different audiences and across time. Christine Letts, senior adviser at the Hauser Institute for Civil Society at Harvard University and Rita E. Hauser senior lecturer in the practice of philanthropy and nonprofit leadership at the Harvard Kennedy School, sees reputation as "what people experience, but the brand as what the organization is projecting." Reputation is certainly important, as it represents cumulative and collective brand image perceptions, but because a brand has both an internal dimension (brand identity) and external dimension (brand image), if you assume that reputation and brand are synonymous, then you are ignoring the internal dimension of brand.

WHAT A BRAND DOES

In the private sector, a brand helps stimulate and sustain the demand for a product or service, through increased awareness and perceived quality. On the customer's side, a brand helps in decision making and building affiliation. A brand also helps build relationships with customers and creates preference, loyalty, and trust. Often a branded product or service is able to charge a price premium, linked to higher perceived quality and loyalty, which in turn results in greater revenues and profitability.

When we asked our interviewees what they believed a strong brand does for a nonprofit organization, there were again some similarities to the private sector, but also some subtle differences. Peter Walker, director of the Feinstein International Center at Tufts University, articulates a commonly held view when he says, "A strong brand allows you to acquire more resources and gives you the authority to have more freedom over how you use them." Brands help in the acquisition of financial, human, and social resources, as well as in forging key partnerships. The trust that strong brands elicit also provides organizations with the authority, credibility, and ability to deploy those resources more efficiently and flexibly than organizations with weaker brands.

In the nonprofit sector, what a brand does for the organization may be more complex. Many nonprofit organizations agree that in addition to their ability to generate resources, their brands also ensure the safety of their personnel in the field, help in the implementation of their missions, provide internal cohesion, and position the organization for potential partnerships (Quelch and Laidler-Kylander, 2005). In her study of UK charities, Hankinson (2005) suggests that the brand also "unifies the workforce around a common purpose; acts as a catalyst for change; and contributes to the professionalism of the sector" (p. 84). She also notes that "the internal brand should work in tandem with the external brand" (p. 90), an idea that is very similar to our concept of brand Integrity and a key aspect of the Role of Brand Cycle, which we review in Chapter Four. Cuesta (2003) suggests that a nonprofit brand "is a value chain that aligns an organization's mission to the results that the board, staff and volunteers create for participants and supporters" (p. 2). Finally, a number of authors have highlighted the multiple audiences that a nonprofit brand must address, which adds to the complexity of branding in the sector.

So are nonprofit brands different from for-profit brands? The answer is both yes and no. We believe that what a brand actually *is* does not differ between sectors, but what a brand *does* for an organization and how it is best managed are quite different. To better understand why the role that a brand plays for a nonprofit organization might be different from a private sector counterpart, and to shed some light on how brand management requirements might also be different, let's turn now to an evaluation of the differences between nonprofits and for-profits more generally and then to how brand management differs between the sectors.

KEY DIFFERENCES BETWEEN FOR-PROFITS AND NONPROFITS

In her seminal work on the management of nonprofit organizations, Oster (1995) suggests that nonprofit organizations differ from their for-profit counterparts in at least five major areas:

1. *Their organizational culture and structure*, which Foreman (1999) confirms is more likely to be based on a consensus-building culture with decentralized structures and with low control by headquarters.

2. *Their employees*, whom Benz (2005) describes as being "intrinsically motivated" and deriving nonfinancial rewards from their work. Benz also confirms that job satisfaction ratings for employees in nonprofit organizations are higher than in for-profit organizations.

3. *A collaborative rather than competitive approach*, which both Liao, Foreman, and Sargeant (2001) and Austin (2000) support. The former argue that "competition has less relevance in the nonprofit arena since demand for goods and services is insatiable" (p. 259); the latter suggests that for nonprofit organizations, collaboration is becoming the rule.

4. *The complexity of their customers*, which makes nonprofit organizations more difficult to manage than for-profits, due in large part to the broader spectrum of stakeholders and brand audiences engaged in both upstream activities (such as fundraising) and downstream activities (such as program implementation) (Letts, Ryan, and Grossman, 1999).

5. *The importance of mission.* Nonprofits lack the common objective shared by for-profit companies, that of making a profit. Instead, they strive to implement a social mission and engage a spectrum of stakeholders. The mission becomes both a goal and a rallying cry.

We add that in the nonprofit sector, there is often a disconnect between the purchaser (donor) of services and products and the user (beneficiary). This disconnect has implications for the brand and the role it must play. Because purchasers cannot experience and evaluate the quality and value of the product or service directly, they must rely on trust to make the "purchase decision" (Laidler-Kylander, Quelch, and Simonin, 2007). We believe that the brand is the vehicle for building this trust.

Finally, whereas for-profit companies are focused on the single metric of profitability, nonprofit organizations are striving for social change that can often be advanced only if other organizations in the field also succeed. In other words, many nonprofits can achieve their goals only with the help of other organizations. The nature of goals in the for-profit and nonprofit sectors is therefore fundamentally and structurally different, and we argue that the role that brand plays in advancing a nonprofit's goals (mission and impact) is more multidimensional and challenging, as is the effective management of that brand, to which we now turn.

TRADITIONAL FOR-PROFIT BRAND MANAGEMENT

Traditional brand management in the private sector can be defined as the collection of activities that go into building, nurturing, and protecting a brand over time (Arnold, 1992). Creating emotional connections with customers as a means of building brand loyalty has become one of the main goals of brand management efforts in the private sector. Positioning as a means of achieving competitive differentiation and increasing visibility and awareness remains one of the main tools of brand management, and more recently, there has been an emphasis on protecting both the brand and brand equity. Developing a clear positioning strategy is a central tenet of brand management. Positioning a brand relative to competitors and targeting specific consumers enable organizations to establish coherent pricing, communications, and product policies in support of that brand (Kapferer, 2002).

Brand management is traditionally viewed as the management of a key asset, albeit an intangible one (Guzman, Montana, and Sierra, 2006). Mitchell (2005) argues that brands are the "tip of complete business ice-bergs" and that although "having a strong brand is indeed crucial for every successful business, brands are not built by a separate activity called 'brand building' any more than races are won by a separate activity called 'winning'" (p. 9). Mitchell defines brand management as consistent, well-targeted, clear communication and believes that the way to manage a brand is to focus on creating and delivering customer value. Strong brands "will follow as a natural result" (p. 8). Thompson and colleagues state that "over the last decade, emotional branding has emerged as a highly influential brand management paradigm" (Thompson, Rindfleisch, and Arsel, 2006, p. 50). Bergstrom, Blumenthal, and Crothers (2002) add that "branding, the verb, is about adding a higher level of emotional meaning to a product or service, thereby increasing its value to customers and other stakeholders" (p. 134). The emotional branding paradigm has, in the private sector, largely replaced the original paradigms based on cognitive theories of consumer knowledge formation (Thompson and others, 2006). Building a brand personality is an extension of this emotional branding paradigm, and much brand research has emphasized the importance of building brand personality in brand management (Fournier, 1998; Johar Venkataramani, Sengupta, and Aaker, 2005; Ogilvy, 1983; Plummer, 1985; Sentis and Markus, 1986).

Over the past decade, there has been a growing trend toward corporate branding, as opposed to product branding, whereby corporate brand management "aims to establish a favorable disposition towards the organization by its various stakeholders" (Gylling and Lindberg-Repo, 2006, p. 257). Knox and Bickerton (2003) define corporate branding as drawing "on the traditions of product branding in that it shares the same objective of creating differentiation and preference" based on positioning. However, these authors believe that corporate branding is "more complex," requiring the management of "interactions with multiple stakeholder audiences" (p. 999). Aaker (2004) also believes that a corporate brand (or organization brand) can "generate leverage, synergy and clarity," which may be particularly useful when the "environment is cluttered, confused, and complex" (p. 6). This shift to corporate branding is particularly interesting and potentially more relevant to nonprofit brand management.

Nurturing and protecting the brand are fundamental brand management tasks in the for-profit sector. Heberden (2002) notes that "lack of investment and skilled management attention tends to result in gradual erosion of brand value, or slower growth than would otherwise be possible" (p. 59). Current research supports investing in brands and emphasizes the importance of protecting the brand. M'zungu, Merrilees, and Miller (2010) suggest that "Brand management ought to play an important role in safeguarding brand equity" (p. 605). Brand protection has to do with the related concepts of consistency and control. For Aaker (1996), consistency of meaning and message over time is one of the most important ways to maintain and protect strong brands. Controlling how the brand is being depicted, by whom and when, as well as being vigilant about the misappropriation or unauthorized use of brand assets (such as logos), help maintain and deliver this consistency in brand meaning and messaging. Many successful for-profit brands aggressively police and control their brand assets, including the use of their taglines and logos. So an important aspect of brand management in the private sector is control and policing with the goal of achieving consistency.

THE LACK OF BRAND MANAGEMENT IN NONPROFITS

Despite the recent publication of a number of books, articles, and blogs on the subject of nonprofit branding, Deatherage (2009) reports that in her recent work with a fairly large and long-established nonprofit organization, only a few people within the organization understood what a brand is and what it can do for them. This experience is shared by a number of our interviewees, who have had to start their brand initiatives with internal discussions and training sessions around the definitions of brand and branding.

Other researchers have found that nonprofits "devote little time, energy and care to branding" (Nissim, 2004) or that they "do not effectively utilize and manage their brands" (Bishop, 2005). Bishop concludes that "brand management is neglected [in nonprofit organizations] because marketing itself is seen as a limited range of activities, mainly concerned with fundraising." This is not surprising, given that a search of the books and articles on the subject of nonprofit brand reveals that more than 70 percent of these publications still emphasize the old paradigm of branding based on fundraising and communications. Ritchie, Swami, and Weinberg (1999) caution that branding can appear to be a source of risk because "brand management can seem commercial, require financial and human resources and can magnify the impact of negative information about an organization" (p. 30).

In our interviews, we frequently encountered negative perceptions and skepticism toward brands and brand management. But we believe that to some extent, this skepticism is anchored in the differences between sectors we noted earlier (Oster, 1995) and a fundamental misunderstanding of brand and the strategic role it can play for nonprofits. The lack of brand management frameworks and tools developed specifically for the nonprofit sector may also have contributed to limited brand management efforts by nonprofit organizations.

Daw and Cone (2011) have helped fill this gap with their book *Breakthrough Nonprofit Branding*. It shows "how a constituency-focused, compelling brand can revolutionize an organization and the way people view and support it" (p. 5). They draw on seven principles: (1) discover the authentic meaning of your brand; (2) embed your brand meaning across the organization; (3) rally internal brand ambassadors; (4) develop 360 communications; (5) expand brand meaning by mobilizing the external community; (6) cultivate partners to extend your brand reach; and (7) leverage your brand for alternative revenue and value. Much of this text aligns with our own work. In particular, making mission and values central to the brand, engaging internal and external stakeholders, and cultivating partners all support our concepts of brand Integrity, brand Democracy, and brand Affinity. Daw and Cone's work also fits directly with the paradigm shift that we discussed in Chapter One and contributes to a new way of thinking about non-profit brands.

HOW DOES THE BRAND IDEA DIFFER FROM TRADITIONAL FOR-PROFIT BRAND MANAGEMENT MODELS?

Brand management models in the private sector largely focus on creating emotional connections with customers as a means of building brand loyalty. Differentiation and positioning are used to establish competitive advantage and to increase awareness and preference in target customer segments. As mentioned earlier, consistency and control have long been the hallmarks of brand protection activities within the traditional for-profit brand management framework. The brand IDEA differs from for-profit brand management in three fundamental ways: first, brand is focused on the mission rather than on consumers; second, positioning is used to gain organizational clarity and to support collaboration rather than to gain competitive advantage; and third, control is replaced by participative engagement. The brand IDEA framework builds on the ideas described in the earlier discussion of the paradigm shift and addresses many of the differences between for-profits and nonprofits we have outlined.

Mission Focus

In the brand IDEA framework, the underlying focus of the brand is the organization's mission and values, as opposed to the customer or end user, which is the focus in traditional for-profit brand management models. That is not to say that a nonprofit's various stakeholders are not important brand audiences. They are. And as we argue in Chapter Four, the brand's role in creating trust, particularly with a range of external stakeholders, is essential. But, at the risk of oversimplifying and generalizing, the goal in for-profit companies is to maximize profitability over the long term. The way to achieve this goal, in many cases, is to create demand from a growing loyal segment of customers. Hence, as we have discussed, the focus of traditional for-profit brand management is on creating and sustaining emotional connections with customers so as to generate profits for the company. For nonprofits, in contrast, the goal is to implement an often complex social mission and to create positive social impact, which requires the help and participation of other organizations. Brand Integrity places the mission, rather than the customer, firmly at the center of the brand. When the brand embodies the mission, values, and strategy of the organization, it also supports the creation of emotional connections, but toward a different end.

Positioning for Clarity

As we have argued, rare is the nonprofit organization that can achieve its mission alone. Increasingly, mission implementation requires building and managing an array of partnerships. The nonprofit brand needs to connect with a range of stakeholders and brand audiences (both internal and external) in order to generate the support and create the collaborative environment necessary to deliver social impact. Fundraising or generating revenue is just part of the picture. Whereas the goal of positioning in for-profit brand management is to achieve competitive advantage, the goal of positioning for nonprofits is to create clarity in brand identity and image and to play a role in identifying partnerships. As Noah Manduke suggests, "Conventional branding does not have a place in nonprofits. There isn't a role for conventional competitive advantage or self-promotion as there is in the private sector."

Brand Affinity highlights the importance of deploying the nonprofit brand in the service of a shared social impact, achieved through collaboration. Brand Affinity represents a radical departure from traditional for-profit brand management. Where for-profit brands strive to gain competitive advantage to achieve the company's internal organizational goal of maximizing profits, nonprofit brands can use positioning to support collaborations focused on driving shared external social goals and collective impact. It becomes less about sharing the pie and more about growing the pie. The focus of the brand in brand Affinity is not about competing for resources but about maximizing impact and achieving the mission through a range of partnerships. Therefore, brand Affinity is fundamentally about using the brand to identify and attract partners and align them behind a shared social objective. As we shall see in later chapters, this implies an open, flexible, and sharing approach to the use of brand assets rather than strict brand policing and control, and a decision to use those brand assets to drive social impact rather than to drive resources and benefits that accrue to a single organization.

Participative Engagement

Brand Integrity aligns mission, values, and strategy with brand identity, and brand identity with brand image, creating a powerful brand. In the brand IDEA framework, this alignment is bidirectional and achieved through brand Democracy, which invites the participation and empowerment of stakeholders. In traditional for-profit brand management models, the brand identity is projected in a systematic fashion by a select few, to create a controlled brand image. Brand Democracy is an approach to brand management that is in stark contrast to and even contradicts the generally accepted practices of brand protection and tight brand control. Brand Democracy advocates the participation of internal and external stakeholders in the development, articulation, and communication of brand identity. Rather than vigilantly controlling all aspects of brand communication, brand Democracy invites participation and is flexible, adaptive, and driven by the rise in collaborative technologies and social media. The process of brand Democracy is as important internally, in developing cohesion and buy-in, as it is externally in influencing brand image. Adopting a brand Democracy approach is a choice that emphasizes authenticity and stakeholder buy-in over the more traditional approaches of control and consistency, and results in a network of brand ambassadors.

Having examined how for-profit and nonprofit brands are managed differently, let's turn now to a discussion of brand equity, or what makes strong brands.

BRAND EQUITY

Brand equity is a measure of the strength of a brand. In the for-profit sector, brand equity is a measure of the brand audience's attachment to the brand. For Aaker (1996), it is "a set of brand assets and liabilities linked to a brand, its name and symbol, that add to or subtract from the value provided by a product or service to that firm's customers" (p. 7). These assets and liabilities can be grouped into five main categories or variables: brand loyalty, name awareness, perceived quality, brand associations, and other assets (such as patents and trademarks). These five variables can be thought of as the drivers of brand equity, and they shed some light on what makes a strong brand in the private sector. It will not come as a surprise at this point that the drivers of brand equity in for-profit and nonprofit brands are different, and this is what we turn to now.

Laidler-Kylander and Simonin (2009) propose an empirical brand equity model for nonprofit organizations that is based on four key drivers. Using a system dynamics approach and grounded theory development through case studies and constant comparison, they elucidate a model in which *trust, partnerships, consistency*, and *focus* drive brand equity in nonprofits. Trust represents the belief held by various stakeholders that the organization will do what it claims to do. Partnerships refer to relationships with business, government, and other nonprofits.

Consistency is defined as organizational consistency in both operations and messaging, across audiences. Focus pertains to the range of operations and the ability of an organization to stick to a specific mission over time. In the system dynamics model, these four interrelated variables are what drive nonprofit brand equity and make brands in the nonprofit sector strong. They also relate closely to the Role of Brand Cycle (described in Chapter Four) and the brand IDEA framework.

Trust

As argued by Bryce (2007), "nonprofit scholars and managers generally recognize that nonprofits need the public's trust for legitimacy, for effectiveness, and for non-financial as well as financial support" (p. 112). As we have discussed, the disconnect that exists between the purchasers and users of nonprofit products and services may account, in part, for the importance of brand trust for many nonprofit organizations (Ritchie and others, 1999; Laidler-Kylander and others, 2007). Trust is built when an organization is truly doing what external stakeholders perceive it to be doing. In the brand IDEA, trust is the result of brand Integrity, where brand identity and image are aligned and where the public's perception (brand image) is aligned with the organization's identity.

Trust is what drives support for the organization and attracts partners. In the system dynamics model developed by Laidler-Kylander, trust is both a precursor and result of successful partnerships; and concentrating efforts on differentiating and positioning the brand enhances this trust, and therefore brand equity. Roehm and Tybout's article (2006) on brand scandal spillovers between competitors in a specific category suggests that scandal spillover effects resulting in the erosion of brand trust are less likely to occur when individual brands within a specific category are well differentiated. This supports our assertion that effective differentiation and positioning can help clarify the organization's brand in the minds of all stakeholders and can help build trust and, as we discuss in Chapter Three, reduce competition in the nonprofit sector.

Partnerships

As we discussed in the Introduction, there has been a tremendous growth in the number and types of partnerships that nonprofits engage in. Salamon (1999, p. 21) depicts a "modern reality of collaborative problem-solving" in the nonprofit field. The nonprofit brand equity model shows that partnerships and relevance are interrelated. The more relevant a brand appears, the more partners it attracts; and the higher the caliber of the partnerships, the more relevant an organization appears to be. We believe that partnerships are essential in terms of both enhancing organizational capacity and enabling an organization to implement its mission and achieve impact. Using brand and brand assets to support partnerships and collaboration is at the heart of the brand Affinity concept.

Consistency

The notion of consistency in brand management is not new. Atilgan, Akinci, Aksoy, and Kaynak (2009) point to consistency and credibility as drivers of brand trust by customers. Consistency of brand image across stakeholders and audiences, over time, and across borders has been declared the "hallmark" of great brands (Fletcher, 2002). Ellis (2004) adds that "maintaining brand consistency across products and locations is the single most important role of the corporate office" (p. 19). Campbell (2002) further argues that the 3Cs of branding are consistency, clarity, and convergence.

In the nonprofit brand equity model, consistency results in both increased trust and visibility. For nonprofit brands with a spectrum of audiences and stakeholders, consistency of brand is more challenging to accomplish but important to achieve. Yasmina Zaidman, director of communications and strategic partnerships at the Acumen Fund, expands on the importance of consistency across audiences: "Brand has to be coherent all the way through, with every conversation, every interaction. I would say consistency means that the brand is the same wherever you look or whomever you speak to. If you're reaching out to an entrepreneur and you're working with them on a potential investment, what they see in our portfolio team is not very different from what a donor experiences at our annual meeting, or from what a potential employee sees during interviews. That consistency is where brand and values overlap." Consistency in the brand IDEA framework is achieved through finding commonality across audiences as part of brand Integrity and through brand Democracy, which engages internal and external stakeholders and provides guidelines and tools rather than a strict policing approach.

Focus

Focus is derived from a strong understanding of differentiation and positioning and is connected to the ability of an organization to stick to the mission in the face of sometimes tempting funding and operational opportunities. Focus is also linked to the notion of simplicity. The more simple an organization's mission and goals, the easier it is to maintain focus. Adamson (2006) advocates for developing a simple "brand idea" that can serve as a rallying cry for employees and customers alike. His brand management approach is based on going back to basics and ensuring alignment with the brand's true meaning.

The nonprofit brand equity model suggests that efforts to increase focus will translate into greater organizational legitimacy and clearer brand positioning. One of the organizations we talked to, Nothing But Nets, provides mosquito nets to fight malaria. The brand and brand name are simple and focused around that one idea. Chris Helfrich, director, attributes the success of the organization and its brand to the fact that "we are who we say we are." Focus plays an important role in bringing clarity to brand identity and brand image and helps achieve brand Integrity, contributing in turn to organizational cohesion and trust.

SUMMARY

In this chapter, we have defined what a brand is and what it does. We believe that although what a brand *is* may be the same across sectors, what a brand can *do* for an organization and how best to manage brands differ between for-profit and nonprofit organizations. These differences are due in part to the fundamental differences between sectors outlined by Oster (1995) and to the paradigm shift we discussed in the previous chapter. Whereas traditional for-profit brand management revolves around creating customer loyalty and policing the use of the brand, the brand IDEA framework we propose rests on three tenets: brand is focused on the mission rather than on consumers; positioning is used to gain organizational clarity and to support collaboration rather than to gain competitive advantage; and control is replaced by participative engagement. Finally, whereas brand equity in the for-profit sector is driven by awareness, loyalty, and perceived quality, nonprofit brand equity is driven by trust, partnerships, consistency, and focus. Figure 2.1 summarizes the main themes discussed in this chapter and compares traditional for-profit brand management to the brand IDEA. In the next chapter, we look at the important concepts of differentiation and positioning, theory of change, and internal branding as they pertain to nonprofit brands.

Traditional For-Profit

Brand

An identifier and concept that imparts information and creates perceptions and emotions

Role of Brand

Drive profitability by stimulating and sustaining the demand for a product or service (often at a premium)

Create preference and loyalty with target customers

Brand Management

Position for competitive advantage

Create emotional connections with customers

Protect and control brand assets

Drivers of Brand Equity

Brand loyalty

Name awareness

Perceived quality

Brand associations

Nonprofit Brand IDEA

Brand

Same! An identifier and concept that imparts information and creates perceptions and emotions

Role of Brand

Implement mission by acquiring and deploying resources

Create trust and organizational cohesion

Brand Management

Position for clarity and collaboration

Create brand ambassadors through participative engagement

Provide guidelines and share brand assets

Drivers of Brand Equity

Trust

Partnerships

Consistency

Focus

FIGURE 2.1. *Differences Between For-Profit Brand Management and the Brand IDEA*

CHAPTER

3

WHAT YOU NEED TO KNOW

Reviewing the Building Blocks of Brand

The concepts of differentiation and positioning are key tenets of strategic marketing and essential precursors to effective brand management. Before you define a brand identity, an analysis of the macro and micro environments, including an assessment of the needs of customers (beneficiaries and funders), forms the basis for differentiation. Positioning is how you communicate that differentiation to create the desired perception, or brand image, relative to other players, in the minds of the target audiences. In this chapter, we explore how the objectives of differentiation and positioning are different in the nonprofit sector. We then look briefly at theory of change and internal branding and how these relate to the brand IDEA framework. Understanding an organization's theory of change enables the organization to explicitly define how it achieves social change; internal branding is an education process that helps stakeholders within the organization build an understanding of brand management concepts. It is these topics—differentiation, positioning, theory of change, and internal branding—that are the fundamental building blocks of brand management in the nonprofit sector.

DIFFERENTIATION AND POSITIONING

Differentiation in the private sector is the emphasis on the specific features of a product or service that lead customers to perceive it as different, desirable, and unique. Positioning builds on this differentiation and positions the product or service relative to competing offerings in the minds of those target audiences that are likely to perceive the most benefit and value the highlighted differences. Marketers often talk about STP, which stands for segmentation, targeting, and positioning. Segmentation is the process of dividing potential customers into segments, targeting is the process of deciding which of the customer segment(s) to focus on, and positioning is the process of communicating the unique benefit of the product or service (relative to competing offerings) to those target customers. In practice, however, successful marketers understand the gaps that exist in current competitor product offerings as well as consumer segment preferences, and they use that knowledge to drive product development efforts. An understanding of the competitive landscape and evolving customer needs is what enables marketers to uncover the unmet needs that give rise to new, differentiated products.

In the nonprofit sector, although some product and service branding does occur, we are mostly concerned with differentiating and positioning organizational brands. We believe that the concepts of differentiation and positioning are as relevant and important (if not more so), although they may be used to a slightly different purpose. To successfully differentiate themselves, nonprofits must have a clear understanding of which beneficiaries and funder segments they want to address, the unmet need they are trying to serve, and what other organizations are doing in their ecosystem. Differentiation and positioning also require an understanding of an organization's own strengths and weaknesses and of any features (values, methodology, aspects of their mission) that make the organization unique. As we shall see later in this chapter, articulating a theory of change to understand how your organization is positioned relative to other players within a broader logic model is an important precursor to differentiation and positioning and can help your organization decide with whom to partner.

The Benefits of Differentiation

Differentiation is what makes an organization unique in its landscape. This uniqueness can stem from the mission itself, the beneficiaries served, the capabilities or expertise the organization has developed, the values espoused, and even the theory of change it believes in.

Differentiation helps an organization stand out in a crowded landscape in a way that is relevant and distinctive. For Noah Manduke, brand differentiation is about "committing to defining your unique significance and rejecting sameness. It's not enough to write a mission statement and be clever marketers or fundraisers. You have to answer the question, What unmet need exists, and how can we meet it in a unique way? In issue areas that are already congested, it can be difficult to avoid duplication and provide unique value."

Differentiation also implies being clear about what an organization is *not* and what it does *not* do. Many nonprofit organizations are loath to do this, as they do not wish to exclude potential supporters or donors. Will Novy-Hildesley, founder of Quicksilver Foundry, noted that "part of the problem is that nonprofit organizations want to be liked by everyone, but powerful brands need to take a stand and be distinctive, sometimes generating powerful emotional reactions." Differentiation requires that an organization be explicit about what it does and does not do and what it believes in, even at the risk of potentially alienating some groups.

Despite the stated importance of brand differentiation, Sargeant and Ford (2007) believe that truly differentiated nonprofits are actually quite rare and that "nonprofits are perceived as a bland homogenous mass of well-meaning but similar organizations with which donors find it hard to bond emotionally and financially" (p. 42). On the one hand, this lack of differentiation means that all nonprofits benefit from a general halo effect that comes simply from being a nonprofit organization. On the other hand, in a world with little differentiation, scandals and unethical behavior at a single nonprofit organization can taint the entire sector and result in negative brand spillover effects. This suggests that being sufficiently differentiated from other nonprofit organizations can become an important form of risk mitigation. And as we explain in the next section, being differentiated from other organizations can actually reduce competitive pressures between nonprofits in the same issue area.

Manduke also expressed concern about the lack of differentiation described by Sargeant and Ford, which he believes is resulting, in part, in an excess of perceived duplication in the nonprofit sector. "The proliferation of nonprofits in North America is intense," he said, "and there is a sea of sameness out there. If there are a hundred like-minded organizations serving the same need, and they are all the same, on what basis do donors choose whom to support? There is a lot of duplicative infrastructure and waste and inefficiency because of lack of market forces and brand stewardship in the social sector."

Effective brand management, based on clear differentiation and positioning, may therefore have a role in addressing this perceived issue of duplication among nonprofits. Again, according to Manduke,

> In the commercial sector when there is commoditization, everyone competes on price, and markets consolidate. But in the social sector, there are no market forces at play that would facilitate consolidation, at least not at the rate of the commercial sector. Without market forces, there isn't pressure to consolidate and focus, or force you out of business if you don't add value. This is why branding plays an important role. Branding is the solution to the commoditization problem because it requires organizations to think through their unique significance and identify how they are going to meet unmet needs in a unique way.

Although addressing the inefficiencies of the nonprofit sector is outside the scope and objectives of this book, it is interesting to note that we are starting to see a greater number of mergers and acquisitions in the nonprofit sector. In Chapter Nine, we touch on mergers and acquisitions and the role the brand IDEA can play in facilitating these activities.

The Importance of Positioning

The most fundamental concept in strategic marketing is, arguably, that of positioning. Positioning, as we have said, is defined as the perception that a target audience holds about a particular product, service, or organization, relative to its competitors. For a nonprofit, it is that "space" you want to occupy in the minds of target audiences and stakeholders, relative to the other players in the field or ecosystem in which you operate. It is how you want to be perceived by your key stakeholders relative to other organizations, in regard to attributes that are of critical importance to them. As Jim Bildner, senior research fellow and adjunct lecturer in public policy at Harvard Kennedy School and trustee of many organizations including the Kresge Foundation and Nonprofit Finance Fund, eloquently stated, "positioning is like a headlight that lets others know where you stand amongst a sea of actors."

Good positioning requires three things: a deep understanding of the needs and wants of the target audiences; a thorough knowledge of other players' strengths and weaknesses; and awareness of one's own organizational strengths and weaknesses, capabilities and capacities, mapped out in relation to others. The approach to positioning espoused by Ries and Trout (2001), who literally wrote the book on positioning, is not necessarily to create something new or different but to "tap into what's already in the mind [of the target audience] and retie the connections that already exist" (p. 5). These authors recommend that researching the landscape and players is an essential first step in successful positioning and that "simple" positioning, based on a single compelling attribute, leads to clarity.

Positioning for Clarity

The Center for Civilians in Conflict began a rebranding initiative in 2011, eight years after its founding. The rebranding effort started with the realization that the organization needed a new name and logo. Executive Director Sarah Holewinski recognized that the original name, the Campaign for Innocent Victims in Conflict, and more important, the frequently used acronym, did not convey the true purpose or current activities of the organization.

With pro bono support from a consulting group, an analysis of the Center's external image among multiple brand audiences led to a breakthrough in the internal understanding of the organization's mission and brand. The consultants created a diagram that reflected the range of issues facing civilians in areas of conflict and the various functions or activities that different organizations provided in this space. This diagram (a version of which is sometimes referred to as a perceptual positioning map) helped the Center clarify its unique value and how the organization fits in the greater ecosystem of related human rights organizations. "This is who we are," explained Holewinski. "We cut right through these other organizations." (See Figure 3.1 for an example of a perceptual positioning map.) In exploring the Center's external image, Holewinski was surprised to learn that the grassroots supporters who had been vital at the inception of the organization were no longer a key audience and had an outdated perception of the Center's brand. It was the military audience who had a "laser-beam focus on who we are."

The clarity that came from an understanding of the nonprofit's external image and positioning relative to other organizations was critical to informing the Center's internal perception of its unique value and identity. Now the mission, identity, and image are all aligned, and the organization has a much better sense of whom it is trying to reach, how, and why. The Center has made its theory of change explicit, and it can directly relate this theory of change to its brand. We believe that for many nonprofits like the Center for Civilians in Conflict, the real benefit of differentiation and positioning stems from the clarity that can be gained from learning how key audiences perceive them and how this informs their own understanding of the unique role they play.

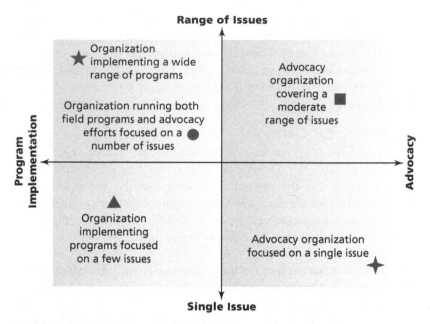

FIGURE 3.1. *Sample Perceptual Positioning Map*

Positioning for clarity, both internally as it relates and feeds into brand identity, and externally in terms of brand image, is one of the key building blocks of brand.

Differentiation and Positioning for Competition or Collaboration?

In the private sector, the objective of differentiation is to competitively position a product or company in the minds of target consumers, so that these consumers will have a preference for one product over another. One of the concerns we heard throughout our interviews was about the notion of competition for funding between nonprofits, which many rejected in favor of operational collaboration. As we mentioned briefly, we believe that it might actually be the lack of differentiation that results in heightened competition in a particular issue area. When the number of organizations in a specific sector is increasing and these organizations are not well differentiated from one another, funders can find it hard to select which organization to support, and everyone potentially competes for the same funding. Similarly, if organizations themselves are unclear

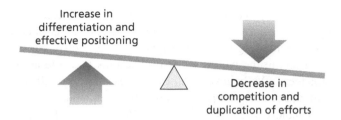

FIGURE 3.2. *The Impact of Differentiation and Positioning on Competition and Duplication in the Nonprofit Sector*

about what their unique contribution is relative to other players, they can be tempted to chase funds that fall outside their scope, which could result in mission creep and increased competition. (This relationship between differentiation and competition is depicted in Figure 3.2.) This concern was voiced by Katherine Fulton, president of the Monitor Institute, who suggested that "the ability to create a clear, distinctive brand identity is ever more important given the increasingly crowded nonprofit landscape."

Lisa Witter, chief change officer at Fenton Communications, encourages her clients to articulate what makes them different from other organizations that are working on the same issues or reaching out to the same donors.

> There has to be real differentiation between you and your competitors, but not in a gladiator sort of way. You have to be really clear about what you do and differentiate yourself and your brand, but that doesn't mean that there's not major collaboration going on. There is or should be. You really need to know what makes you different from other organizations in the same space. Donors want to know how you are different or better—and they like to see collaboration. Understanding what is your differentiator also helps you identify who your partners should be.

Witter believes that effective differentiation enhances collaboration. "Now more than ever," she emphasized, "there has to be collaboration. Collaboration is currency. You have to be very clear about what you do within the collaborative and competitive landscape. Sometimes that analysis leads organizations to do different, complementary things." Witter goes on to argue that effective differentiation is also a precursor to collaboration. "Brand differentiation helps internal constituents and external partners clearly understand the unique role or set of competencies that a particular organization brings to the collective table, clarifying and facilitating the whole set of interactions and role assignments within alliances." We believe that in this way, effective differentiation and positioning reduce competition and enhance collaboration.

Sasha Chanoff, founder and CEO of RefugePoint, has an interesting approach to this issue of competition versus collaboration. Chanoff knows all the players in his issue area, and he considers them broadly as partners. When he is approached by a funder interested in funding a particular program that falls outside RefugePoint's mission and unique focus, Chanoff will say, "We don't really do that, but I know who does, and I can put you in touch with them." In this way, Chanoff maintains his mission focus while at the same time promoting and channeling funding to other players that might be considered competitors. He is able to do this because he has great clarity in terms of his organization's positioning strategy and theory of change. These efforts create a more collaborative atmosphere and increase impact overall in the sector.

INTERRELATION OF BRAND, POSITIONING, AND DIFFERENTIATION

Differentiation, positioning, and brand management are closely related to strategy and are mutually reinforcing. Understanding differentiation enables an organization to effectively position itself relative to other players in the minds of its target audiences, which results in a unique brand identity and image. The brand then reflects the positioning strategy and communicates and enhances an organization's perceived differentiation. As we have said, successful positioning depends on a thorough understanding of the external environment and stakeholder needs, as well as how these are changing and why. Being or becoming the organization of choice to meet a specific target audience's defined needs is one of the goals of positioning and helps ensure that the organization and its brand remain relevant. The brand becomes the vehicle for communicating and reflecting the positioning strategy, which in turn reinforces differentiation. Because differentiation and positioning influence both brand identity and image, they are the building blocks of brand Integrity, which seeks to achieve alignment between identity and image.

The positioning strategy is often the starting point for any brand or rebranding initiative. Shokay, which means "yak yarn" in Tibetan, is a social enterprise working with local yak herders in Western China. Shokay sources yak fibers from the herders, then outsources combing and spinning to create fine yarn and produce luxury finished products, reinvesting revenues into community development for the yak herders. Initially, the organization focused just on selling the yarn itself, but over time, Carol Chyau, Shokay's founder and CEO, recognized that to have a greater impact, the organization needed to change its strategy and create a broader demand for yak fibers. She explained, "In order to maximize our impact on the yak herder communities, we have to work on generating as much demand as possible, and that cannot come from sales of our own products alone. Our goal is therefore to generate demand for yak fiber textiles more broadly and to create a perception of quality similar to that of cashmere. In order to accomplish our goal, successful branding is essential." The organization needed to position itself as a credible player in the fashion industry and develop partnerships with luxury retailers and distributors. "This influenced our decision to rebrand," described Chyau. "Our new brand is more sophisticated and works better when used alongside other luxury brands. We are on par with our retail and designer partners." The social mission remains very much part of the organization's differentiation and brand identity, but the desire to fit with key strategic partners has influenced how the brand image has evolved.

Positioning also enables an organization to understand how it fits into a broader theory of change and with whom it might make sense to partner and collaborate. By understanding who else is providing similar services or focusing on similar target beneficiaries (but providing complementary services) organizations can identify where the overlaps are and with whom collaboration might increase overall impact. So positioning is also a building block for brand Affinity and the use of brand to promote and support collaborations.

THEORIES OF CHANGE

Theories of change, or logic models, are tools that help nonprofit organizations map out the steps that they believe are required to lead to the social impact they hope to achieve. They describe the inputs, activities, and assumptions by which the outputs and outcomes will be achieved, such as through changes in attitudes, knowledge, awareness, skills, behavior, health, family stability, and financial status. Articulating a detailed theory of change is increasingly important for all nonprofit organizations, not only in terms of strategy and resource allocation decisions, but also in terms of monitoring and evaluating their program and organizational effectiveness (Thomas, 2010). By being explicit about the assumptions underlying their theory of change, and using a developmental approach to building the theory of change, as Brest (2010) recommends, organizations can also use theory of change as a vehicle for organizational learning. As we mentioned earlier, theories of change can also help organizations think about positioning both in terms of themselves and in terms of identifying potential partners.

We believe that the brand plays a role at each step in the theory of change, addressing different audiences and forging the relationships necessary to ensure the implementation of the mission. Thus issues of differentiation and positioning also arise at each step in the theory of change. Julie O'Brien, vice president of communications and knowledge exchange at Management Sciences for Health, talked clearly about the role of the brand in the series of activities that enable the organization to achieve impact. She noted that a strong brand can help an organization access and mobilize much-needed resources at each step to achieve the overarching goal.

Defining an organizational theory of change requires clarifying assumptions and describing the explicit mechanisms through which programs and services lead to outcomes. For example, the Center for Civilians in Conflict articulates how they effect change by working with military leaders engaged in war, providing policies and operating procedures to minimize the impact of conflict on civilians. More detailed descriptions of how they work with military leaders, how they develop these policies and procedures, and how they improve life for civilians define their theory of change further.

At each step in the theory of change, it is important to define the role of key players by asking the following two questions:

1. Is our organization in the best position to accomplish this step, or can it be done better by someone else? (If so, by whom?)

2. What role does the brand play in this step? Who is the target audience, and how might the brand be positioned to more effectively reach or communicate with this audience?

Answers to the first question can help ascertain the unique characteristics and differentiating features of an organization, those that make it the most relevant or effective player for a particular step in the theory of change. It can also help identify which partnerships and collaborations could be developed in order to accomplish a particular step that might be beyond the organization's expertise or ability. Rather than creating new capabilities, an organization can look to existing players to fill specific steps in the theory of change. This helps address the problem of duplication in the sector that we touched on earlier. If a particular step in the theory of change can be more effectively and efficiently accomplished by working with or through another organization, this can be taken into account in the organization's strategic decision-making process. Answers to the second question help the organization reflect on the multiple audiences that a nonprofit brand must reach, and how both differentiation and positioning strategies should be formulated to address them.

Jumpstart, for example, is a national early education nonprofit organization providing one-on-one support to preschool children in low-income neighborhoods, with the objective of getting them ready for school and closing the achievement gap. Jumpstart's theory of change is that by identifying preschoolers who are falling behind their peers and intervening early at an individual level in a customized way and with well-trained tutors, children will be more academically and socially ready to start school and better positioned for academic success later in life (Grossman and McCaffrey, 2001). Jumpstart partners with universities and AmeriCorps to recruit college student volunteers who serve as tutors. It partners with Head Start to access beneficiaries and deliver services by providing its programs at Head Start locations. Finally, the organization partners with HighScope to access the best curriculum and volunteer training materials. At each step in Jumpstart's theory of change, the organization has sought to use existing resources and organizations (with expertise and experience) rather than duplicate efforts. This has enabled Jumpstart to focus on developing an operational system based on extensive monitoring and evaluation metrics, one that delivers excellent training to its volunteers in support of its education mission. This activity, in essence, is its unique positioning and differentiated value. Similarly, the Jumpstart brand addresses multiple audiences at different stages in the theory of change. It engages a broad range of donors, volunteers, nonprofit partners, governmental agencies, parents, legislators, and school districts. Each of these brand audiences plays a specific role at different points in Jumpstart's theory of change.

Understanding which partners are crucial at which step in the theory of change, as well as how the brand supports each audience at each step, is fundamental to effective positioning and to maximizing the impact a nonprofit brand can have in implementing its mission. Partnering with those organizations that sit both upstream and downstream in the theory of change can also help a nonprofit more clearly define its own role and unique relevance relative to other players, and understand how best to work with these players to drive common social impact and reduce redundancy in the sector. In this way, theory of change becomes a building block for brand Integrity as well as brand Affinity.

Having described how theory of change can help an organization think about its distinctive role relative to other players, connect with key audiences, and identify potential partners, we now turn to a more internal focus and a discussion of the importance of internal branding for nonprofit organizations.

INTERNAL BRANDING

Internal branding has become a hot topic in marketing (Bobula, 2005). It can be defined as focusing brand activities on internal audiences, such as board members, employees, and volunteers, in order to create a consistent internal perception of the brand. Vallaster (2004) also notes that internal branding creates a "coherent brand understanding among employees from different cultural backgrounds" (p. 100). Bergstrom, Blumenthal, and Crothers (2002) have identified three aspects of successful internal branding: "communicating the brand effectively to the employees; convincing them of its relevance and worth; and successfully linking every job in the organization to the delivery of the brand essence" (p. 135).

In the private sector, internal branding is particularly important for service companies, whose customers both expect and value consistency in the experience and quality of service they receive. Great service organizations understand that their employees represent one of the main brand touchpoints for their customers and that achieving consistency in service delivery will promote trust and a preference for that organization's services with their target customers. Internal branding is one of the vehicles for achieving this consistency, and employees are all trained and coached to communicate about the organization and its brand in a particular manner.

For nonprofits, internal branding is also important and is a key precursor of the larger concept of brand Democracy. An important aspect of internal branding is to promote alignment between the internal and external brand, which we refer to as brand identity and brand image in the brand IDEA framework, and which results in brand Integrity. Burmann and Zeplin (2005) support this and suggest that a strong brand requires alignment between the desired and actual brand identities and the outside perception of the brand. Internal branding is therefore a building block for both brand Integrity and brand Democracy.

As we shall see in the next chapter, the brand plays a particularly important role internally for nonprofit organizations. For nonprofits with decentralized organizational structures and consensus-building cultures, the role of the brand internally in creating consistency and cohesion through this alignment may be as important, if not more important, than the external role of the brand (Foreman, 1999). Although internal branding and education are starting points for brand Democracy, they still tend to rely on a one-way communication process, whereas brand Democracy advocates taking internal branding one step further and promoting more participative engagement through dialogue.

SUMMARY

In this chapter, we covered the building blocks of nonprofit brand management: differentiation and positioning; theory of change; and internal branding. We argue that for nonprofit organizations, the benefits of differentiation and positioning lie in the clarity that an organization gains from understanding the unique role it plays in an ecosystem; this clarity helps crystallize brand identity and image and promotes collaboration. Differentiation and positioning are therefore key building blocks of brand Integrity, brand Affinity, and brand Democracy. It should be noted that positioning requires a good understanding of beneficiary needs; the strengths and weaknesses of other organizations in the sector; and a realistic understanding of one's own organizational capacities and capabilities. Articulating a theory of change sheds additional light on the roles of different actors in an ecosystem, and can help an organization identify its unique role and at which point(s) collaboration might be

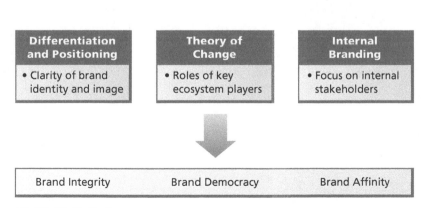

FIGURE 3.3. *The Building Blocks of Nonprofit Brand and the Brand IDEA Framework*

helpful in implementing the overall mission. Theory of change is there-fore a building block of both brand Integrity and brand Affinity. Finally, we introduced the notion of internal branding and argue that it can be particularly important for nonprofit organizations. Internal branding is a building block of brand Integrity through brand Democracy. The relationship between the three building blocks of brand and the elements of the brand IDEA framework are depicted in Figure 3.3.

CHAPTER

WHY THE SKEPTICS HAVE IT WRONG

Understanding the Role and Benefits of Brand

In the preceding chapters, we have introduced the brand IDEA framework, defined key terms around brand and brand management and discussed how these differ between sectors, and introduced the building blocks of differentiation and positioning, theory of change, and internal branding. In this chapter, we will examine the Role of Brand Cycle, which summarizes the benefits of brand management in the nonprofit sector. First, however, we shall explore the sources of skepticism toward brands in the nonprofit sector and revisit the paradigm shift we introduced in Chapter One. Then we shall expand on both the internal and external benefits derived from a strong brand and highlight how these are achieved through brand management using the brand IDEA framework.

SKEPTICISM OF BRAND AND BRAND MANAGEMENT

When we started to conduct our research two years ago, close to 50 percent of our interviewees expressed some degree of ambivalence toward brands and the use of brand management in the nonprofit sector. This skepticism centered on five main concerns: commercialism, ethical concerns, pushback from the organization, vanity of leadership, and the impact of brands on partnerships. We shall take a look at each of these in turn.

Commercialism

Many nonprofit managers we talked with expressed the concern that brand and brand management, when seen primarily as tools for raising money and embodied by a "marketing approach," were fundamentally at odds with the values of the nonprofit sector. "I believe it is the word *branding* that people are the most 'allergic' to," explained Julie Jung, director of communications at the University of Chicago School of Social Service Administration. For many, the word itself evokes images of advertising and sales, which are not considered a good fit for those working in the nonprofit sector. As Julie O'Brien of Management Sciences for Health noted, "our staff equated branding with marketing, and there was a strong feeling that since the organization was mission driven, 'marketing' was both distasteful and irrelevant."

Christine Letts of Harvard Kennedy School shared her concerns about the way some relief organizations focus on fundraising at the expense of engaging and educating the public on their work in a more transparent and meaningful way. "They are primarily visible in the middle of disasters and when they are asking for money," she explained, "and so the brand becomes associated only with capital-enhancing activities in the middle of disasters, and then they are never heard from again." Letts sees this as a process of "exploiting" the brand instead of "building" the brand through communicating, consistently and transparently, who the organization is and what it does.

Dr. Wibulpolprasert, senior adviser at Thailand's Ministry of Health, is not alone when he questions whether the nonprofit sector is spending too much money on PR and communications at the expense of doing the work that actually benefits society. When the brand is narrowly defined around fundraising and PR, then investing in building and managing the brand is often seen as an unnecessary expense.

Will Novy-Hildesley framed this concern about commercialism in the following way: "People have a lot of misgivings about the idea of branding because they tend to conflate it with advertising. Seen through that lens, right off the bat, you have a considerable uphill struggle to get people in nonprofits to think about branding differently, more strategically. As soon as they see the word 'branding,' they shift to a commercial mindset." This view of the brand as a tool or lever for commercial gain is very different from our new paradigm in which the brand is a strategic asset for implementing the mission.

Ethical Concerns

We also heard concerns around sacrificing one's ethics and respect for others' dignity in the effort to raise money and increase revenue. Peter Bell, senior research fellow at the Hauser Institute for Civil Society at Harvard University and former CEO of CARE, acknowledged that "NGOs who still put the infomercials on television showing fly-speckled children may be 'successful' in fundraising, but the approach is disrespectful to those children and detrimental to advancing the effectiveness of humanitarian organizations more broadly." Others, such as Mahnaz Afkhami, founder and president of Women's Learning Partnership, suggested that what sells in fundraising can often be in direct tension and contradiction with the type of local empowerment efforts that most INGOs aim to foster. "Selling your ideas the way you sell cereal, in campaigns such as 'save a slave' or 'adopt a rape victim,' have been common practices in some INGOs, but can be, I believe, detrimental to your cause."

Other interviewees highlighted an example in Haiti, where the pressure to brand resulted in all the donated latrines' bearing nonprofit logos. Examples of the use of brand in this way are considered by many people to be at odds with the fundamental values of the sector and bordering on distasteful. In these cases, the brand is seen as a PR or promotional tool with the sole objective of raising awareness, visibility, and financial support for a specific organization.

Pushback

Brand management processes, and rebranding exercises in particular, are fairly visible and can result in organizational pushback, creating a challenging and at times contentious environment. John Quelch, Charles Edward Wilson Professor of Business Administration at Harvard Business School, described the branding process as a lightning rod:

> There is often tension around branding and rebranding efforts. When people see changes occurring in an organization that they are uncomfortable with, they may seize upon the brand as something to defend in reaction to broader organizational changes. When a new CEO arrives, he or she may want to redefine the organization's strategy, and as part of that process, the logo, for example, might get updated. Changes in logo elicit a lot of (often) negative reactions. Logos and taglines are very visible and represent important connections for people. So changes in logos can act like a lightning rod through which cumulative grievances over other issues can be channeled.

We see here that rebranding initiatives are often experienced as top-down efforts to change organizations without participation or consultation. The natural reaction is to resist this change, and the logo can become a symbolic fighting ground.

Vanity

This issue was mentioned as a concern primarily in the case of foundations, when the rationale for the branding process was unclear or perceived to be driven by issues other than organizational capacity building. Katherine Fulton, of the Monitor Institute, noted that "too many foundations have approached the brand question in a purely ego-driven manner, driven by either the CEO or the board or the founder. I've seen situations where the brand, the reputation, has become an end in itself, or just too personal to the leadership, rather than a tool for fulfilling the mission." When this happens, skepticism around brand management increases both within the organization and on the part of external stakeholders. Steve Lawry, senior research fellow at the Hauser Institute for Civil Society at Harvard University, also suggested that brand management can be profoundly influenced and driven by senior leadership as a form of self-expression, which can exacerbate the organizational resistance to the brand management process and create pushback throughout the organization.

Impact on Partnership

The final concern skeptics may have, particularly in organizations that increasingly work in coalitions and collaborations, is that one organization's powerful brand will overshadow weaker brands, reinforcing, rather than alleviating, imbalances of power among partners. Brand visibility can take precedence over partnership goals, creating unequal relationships and possibly resulting in brand confusion. As Ramesh Singh, former chief executive of ActionAid and formerly with Open Society Foundations, noted, "There's a tension between bigger brands and smaller brands. The bigger international NGOs and philanthropies can sometimes push their own brand more, to the detriment of other organizations that can become invisible, and it's always resented." Christian Teriete, communications director at the Global Campaign for Climate Action, who worked on the coalition TckTckTck, indicated that before a collective strategy was decided on, brand colleagues from different organizations were all promoting their own logos on collective products. "It amounted to a 'logo salad,'" recalled Teriete, "and was hardly a strategic practice." The resulting confusion arising from this approach diminished the overall collaborative endeavor and its ability to create impact.

Rather than dismissing these sources of skepticism, we take them seriously and understand that they are rooted in the limited and outdated view of brand as a fundraising and PR tool.

REVISITING THE PARADIGM SHIFT

When the brand is primarily perceived to be a fundraising tool, it makes sense to push for increased external visibility and awareness whenever possible, because that is what will increase the flow of funds to the organization. Indeed, that is what traditional for-profit brand management models, focused on increasing profitability, would advocate. But in the new paradigm, nonprofit brands play key internal and external roles. Donors become only one of a number of internal and external stakeholders or brand audiences that the brand must address. This shift, as we have mentioned, involves a change in both the perception of the role of the brand and how the brand might best be managed.

If the five areas of concern or skepticism we've described are viewed in light of this paradigm shift, they no longer seem as potent. In the new paradigm, the objectives shift from fundraising to mission implementation, and the brand is viewed as a strategic asset that embodies the mission and values of the organization, with the purpose of creating support and partnerships to achieve social impact. In fairness, many excellent nonprofit managers tasked with marketing and fundraising for their organizations are already embedding mission in their brand discussions and focusing on building relationships rather than driving financial transactions. Indeed, it is from these strategic (or exponential) fundraisers that we have learned, and we have incorporated their wisdom into the brand IDEA framework.

Carving out a new path for brand management away from the "commercial" approach, Stephanie Kurzina, vice president of development and communications at Oxfam America, noted that "we shouldn't just be dashing off to rent billboards or do advertising on the T [the Boston subway]. If you can help people understand how their donations contribute to growth and expanding our ability to execute the mission, then they want to support the work. That's the goal of communication and branding." The emphasis is therefore less on getting the donation and more about generating support and understanding of the mission. In this way, the concern about commercialism is substantially reduced, as brand is no longer just about the money. Fundraising becomes a means to an end, not an end in itself. Concurrently, as Jennifer McCrea suggested, "Fundraising is about building relationships and developing advocates and partners for the organization and its goals." This longer-term view of fundraising is anchored in developing partnerships around the organization's mission and goals. Focusing on the mission and the social impact can reduce the potential discomfort around commercialism.

When brand embodies the mission and values, there is also less potential for dissonance between how the brand is used or deployed and the values that the brand embodies. The mission and social impact become integrated into the brand, and the brand becomes a source of pride and passion for everyone connected to the organization. The brand is expressed and used in ways that are consistent with the mission and that mirror the organization's ethics and values, thereby reducing the potential for ethical concerns in communications.

The next two concerns, pushback and vanity, have to do with brand management itself. Brand management is sometimes perceived as a process imposed by organizational leadership without a strong rationale or logic. As we stated earlier, when changes to the brand are imposed from above and the use of brand assets and communications are tightly controlled and policed, organizational pushback can occur. Change, particularly when it is visible, nonparticipatory, and perceived as unnecessary or having negative consequences, creates organizational pushback and skepticism around both the validity and impact of brand management. In the paradigm shift, the process of brand management, from defining the brand to articulating and communicating it, involves broad participation and engagement of both internal and external stakeholders, who then become brand ambassadors. As a result of this participation, or brand Democracy approach, the brand is no longer the controlled reflection of a small number of individuals at the top of the organization. Pushback and vanity are less likely to occur when people are actively engaged in a participative approach to brand management.

Finally, the concern that brand has a negative impact on partnerships is connected both to the narrow view of brand as a tool for fundraising and generating organizational visibility, and to the focus on positioning for competitive advantage. If we again consider the new nonprofit brand paradigm, we find that brand positioning is driven not by the need for competitive advantage but by the desire to clarify, identify, promote, and leverage partnerships that will help implement the mission and drive social impact. The shift in the role of positioning dissipates the concerns we heard around the negative impacts of brand on partnerships.

Understanding the benefits that can be gained from embracing brand and brand management can also help overcome skepticism and reticence. These benefits are described more fully in the Role of Brand Cycle, to which we now turn.

THE ROLE OF BRAND CYCLE

The Role of Brand Cycle, depicted in Figure 4.1, illustrates the critical role a nonprofit brand plays in creating cohesion and trust, which result in capacity and impact. Nonprofit brands play both internal and external roles. In fact, as we noted earlier, the internal role of brand is particularly important for nonprofit organizations. Internally, a clear brand identity creates cohesion within the organization, which results in increased organizational capacity. Cohesion and capacity are the internal benefits, the "goodies," that strong brands bring to their organization. Externally, a clear brand image results in trust and impact, which can be thought of as the external benefits that strong brands bring. In the Role of Brand Cycle, we highlight the fact that brand management is nested within an

FIGURE 4.1. *The Role of Brand Cycle*

organization's strategy, which in turn is derived from the organization's mission and values.

Many of the organizations we spoke with have connected their strategic planning processes with work on their brand. In some cases, the decision to rebrand was the result of strategic planning; in others, work on the brand led to a reassessment of the organization's mission and strategy. Organizations that we have seen rebrand successfully have closely linked their branding and strategy processes.

Cohesion

As we discussed in earlier chapters, the brand identity of an organization incorporates both its mission and values. A strong brand identity means having a clear sense of who the organization is, what it does, and why it matters. Pip Emery, former head of brand identity/communications at Amnesty International, believes that in order to have a strong, relevant brand, "you need to know who you are, where you are going and why you are relevant" (Stone, 2011, p. 4). A focused brand identity, understood and shared by everyone internally, is what creates cohesion for the organization. This is the case for Twaweza, whose brand is captured in the Swahili phrase "Ni Sisi!" meaning, "It's us!" emphasizing that sustainable change happens only if the citizens are behind it. Kees de Graaf, Twaweza's management coordinator, described the power of the brand as follows: "Everything we do is 'Ni Sisi!' It's very cohesive in our organization. This principle is at the heart of the organization." Staff at Twaweza have embraced this notion and understand the organization and its mission.

When an organization's employees and volunteers across functional areas and geographies all embrace a common brand identity, it creates organizational cohesion, builds focus, and reinforces shared values and a common understanding that help drive consistent decision making across the organization. As Marcia Marsh, chief operating officer of the World Wildlife Fund (WWF) in the United States, put it, "Our brand is the single greatest asset that our network has, and it's what keeps everyone together" (Jayawickrama, 2011, p. 6). Because many organizations are composed of different entities, programs, and departments working fairly autonomously, brand identity can create a sense of common objectives and establish a shared bond, building cohesion in sometimes disparate organizational structures.

When internal branding and a participative approach such as brand Democracy is used to develop and articulate brand identity, the benefits in terms of internal cohesion are compounded. A shared understanding for the entire organization can result, such that everyone sees that he or she is working toward the same goal, and the actions of individuals, departments, and programs are aligned. Cohesion enables organizations to make better, more consistent decisions more efficiently and more effectively. Anchoring the brand in the mission, values, and strategy helps solidify this shared understanding and shared commitment, which can also contribute to a stronger organizational culture and better morale. Meghan Reddick, vice president of communications at YMCA Canada, explained that by using a participative process, "Brand is a kind of vehicle for organizational cohesion, for building collective capacity. One of the benefits of our brand refresh, which included internal education and training, has been the growth in dialogue and exchange between the fifty-one independent YMCA member associations."

This internal role of the brand in nonprofits cannot be underestimated and requires that the organization embrace internal branding and the use of a brand Democracy approach. As we shall see in Chapter Six, achieving cohesion through brand Democracy is no mean feat and requires time, energy, and a good deal of patience.

Trust

Externally, brand image, particularly when it is strongly aligned with brand identity, creates trust, enabling the organization to more effectively implement the mission and generate impact. Brand image is a reflection of the variety of perceptions held in the minds of the organization's multiple stakeholders, built on their experiences, interactions, and communications with the organization. This includes not just donors and supporters but also partners, beneficiaries, and those external stakeholders an organization seeks to influence, assist, or reach.

Consistent and compelling brand image and positioning create trust among these multiple external audiences. As Tom Scott, director of global brand and innovation at the Bill & Melinda Gates Foundation, explained, "To be really successful in the work that we do, and this is true for everyone, whether you're selling a product, promoting an issue, or raising money, trust is the most important attribute. Audiences have to trust that your motivations are what you say they are." As we have mentioned before, understanding the drivers of trust is particularly important for nonprofits, where many stakeholders (such as donors) may not themselves directly experience the product or service. Nonprofits must rely on establishing trust with these different external audiences in order to effectively implement their mission and drive impact. An additional benefit of establishing trust with key stakeholders is that it can speed up decision-making processes with donors and partners. Jennifer Benito-Kowalski, director of outreach for Save the Redwoods League, described how the brand helps build trust and support for the organization: "Our brand helps people understand and brings them along with how and what we do to protect redwood forests and their supporting landscapes." Because nonprofit organizations rely on establishing trust with many external audiences, doing what you say you do and being who you say you are, are crucial.

Capacity

Both internal cohesion and external trust contribute to building greater organizational capacity. A cohesive organization uses its existing resources and assets more efficiently, making better decisions and leveraging the whole of its organizational capacity to increase impact. External trust draws people, funds, and partners to the organization, thereby increasing the organization's capacity and ability to implement its programs.

Many of our interviewees agree that a strong brand will attract, recruit, and retain talented staff or volunteers who share similar values and want to be a part of the mission of the organization. The brand can also bring increased financial resources to the organization, and we believe that relationships and partnerships can be viewed as important organizational assets that also contribute to building capacity. Ramesh Singh reflected on how the brand invites relationships that help further ActionAid's mission:

> I understand branding from two sides of the coin. One is the identity, which is the inside of the coin, and [the other is] the profile, which is the external. That they are very interrelated allows us to focus, to be brave, and to speak out. And because we were doing [this], we have more different kinds of organizations and movements (feminist movements, peasant movements) willing to work with us, join hands, and develop a campaign than we would otherwise . . . [Branding] has invited relationships from people, organizations, and movements without which we wouldn't otherwise have been able to work.

In our opinion, the most important assets a brand can help attract are people and relationships, both of which require trust. It is through these people and relationships that financial resources can flow.

Impact

Mission impact is the end goal. By leveraging internal capacity and the trust of partners, beneficiaries, and policymakers, an organization can more effectively implement its programs and activities and achieve its mission objectives, thereby increasing its impact. As Marta Tellado, vice president of global communications at the Ford Foundation, summarized, "A brand can be a powerful tool or framework that helps create deeper impact. A brand can build trust, relevance, support, and understanding of a complex mission." Impact is what an organization achieves when it successfully implements its mission, and what helps create credibility and legitimacy in the eyes of external constituents. Dr. Wibulpolprasert suggests that a brand is strengthened in a virtuous social capital cycle, whereby positive outcomes and experiences with a variety of partners or customers result in an increase in social capital, which strengthens the organization's ability to more efficiently and effectively draw partners, implement its mission, and achieve impact.

Closing the Cycle

Brand management is a journey rather than a destination. The Role of Brand Cycle is completed, and started anew, when the organization reflects back on how its internal capacity, including organizational learning, has evolved, and this provides new input to its brand identity. Changes in the external environment, as well as organizational growth and life-cycle shifts, lead to the evolution of the internal identity over time. Similarly, the experiences that external stakeholders have with the organization and its work or impact are reflected in the legitimacy and credibility gained, and these help shape the brand image over time. As constituents experience the brand through an array of touchpoints and experiences, their perceptions can confirm or influence changes to both internal brand identity and external brand image.

SUMMARY

We started this chapter by exploring the sources of skepticism toward brand and brand management in the nonprofit sector: commercialism, ethical concerns, pushback, vanity, and impact on partnerships. We believe that this skepticism is largely rooted in the old brand paradigm and resistance to private sector models and terminology. We ended this chapter by describing the Role of Brand Cycle, in which brand plays both internal and external roles. Strong brands, whose identity and image are clear and aligned, give rise to organizational cohesion and trust. These in turn result in increased capacity and ability to achieve impact. Over time, capacity and impact influence both brand identity and image, and the cycle continues.

This chapter concludes Part One of our book. We hope that it has provided a useful background and context with which to better understand the brand IDEA. In the following chapters, we explore each of the brand IDEA components in depth and describe how the framework fits together.

2

GETTING THE BRAND IDEA

CHAPTER

5

BRAND INTEGRITY

We have laid the groundwork for understanding the foundational concepts of brand and the role a brand can play in nonprofits, including the benefits that a strong brand can bring to an organization. We turn now to the specifics of the brand IDEA. In this chapter, we discuss brand Integrity, which refers to the alignment between the brand identity and image and the mission, values, and strategy of the organization. Brand identity and brand image are two sides of the same coin: brand identity is the internal reflection of the organization's brand; brand image is the external perception of that same organization's brand. When these are aligned with each other and with the mission, values, and strategy, they contribute to greater organizational cohesion, trust, capacity, and impact, as we discussed in Chapter Four. This chapter examines these topics, as well as the role of multiple audiences, how brand Integrity can support decision making, and the challenges in achieving brand Integrity.

A good brand portrays the unique significance or value proposition of the organization and positions it in relation to other players. The principle of brand Integrity builds on this concept of differentiation and positioning to achieve alignment first between the identity and the organization's mission, values, and strategy, and then between the internal identity and the external image.

Many of our interviewees talked about elements of brand Integrity, and we quote them throughout the chapter to bring this concept to life.

BRAND IDENTITY

When the brand is anchored in the mission, values, and strategy as we suggest, brand identity encapsulates the essence of the organization. Will Novy-Hildesley shared the following concept, which comes originally from Greg Galle of Creative Capital:

Brand identity answers three key questions:

1. Who you are
2. What you do
3. Why does it matter

Capturing the "who, what, and why" of an organization in the internal identity of the brand reflects the paradigm shift from viewing the brand as a communications or fundraising tool focused on the donor to viewing it as a strategic asset focused on implementing the mission. When the brand is anchored in the mission, values, and strategy, the identity becomes the internal reflection or collective perception of everyone in the organization, and captures the very nature or raison d'être of the organization itself.

This view of the brand as representing something fundamental to the organization was echoed in many of our interviews. Brand identity was described as a "mirror," the "soul and essence," and the "spirit and persona" of an organization. Yasmina Zaidman of Acumen Fund described her understanding of brand identity as follows: "The brand is really our identity and our story. It is the ephemeral but essential thing about us, what is true about us." Laura Sanchez, former senior associate for strategic communications and engagement at Living Cities (and current digital strategist at Atlantic Media Strategies), expanded on this concept and said that "Brand is the essential first step for helping people understand the organization."

Tom Scott of the Bill & Melinda Gates Foundation discussed the importance of using the brand to convey the what, how, and why of the organization. "It's really hard to just have the 'what' and the 'how.' You also need to get the 'why' part right and articulate why you're doing what you're doing and why it matters, and why you've made the choices that you've made. The 'why' is more the emotional connection with your audiences, and you need a mix of emotional and rational when people are making decisions about you."

Brand identity is also aspirational in nature. Defining brand identity is itself a journey that conveys both who the organization currently is and where it hopes to be in the future. Any branding process needs to start with a clear sense of identity. For Chris van Dyke, former senior vice president of strategic communications at the World Wildlife Fund, "You need self-awareness and a real, clear view of who you are and where you're headed. Organizations that are attempting to create brands that don't have a clear view of who they are and where they're headed are going to have a very hard time creating a relationship that can result in exerting influence and bringing change. Great brands are built from the inside out."

In addition to conveying the who, what, and why of an organization, the brand identity can also link to organizational culture, history, and institutional memory. Marta Tellado of the Ford Foundation found an internal brand exercise helpful to "tap in to our own collective consciousness about who we are and what is being conveyed, right down to fundamental things like what are our greatest accomplishments. After seventy-five years, it takes some work to keep track of the shared sense of accomplishment about what has been achieved. It's the organization's responsibility to harvest and make use of that institutional memory to its full extent. A brand is much more powerful when it is informed by our legacy and record of accomplishment." Defining a clear brand identity is therefore a critical first step in building a strong brand.

EMBEDDING IDENTITY WITHIN STRATEGY

An organization's brand needs to be considered in conjunction with the strategy of the organization. As Tellado explained, "You can't communicate effectively unless you have strategic focus." We talked to a number of organizations whose work on brand identity was aligned with their strategic planning efforts. In 2005, Anne Goddard's first task as president and CEO of Childfund (formerly Christian Children's Fund) was to develop a new strategy and a plan to change the name of the organization, which focuses on helping vulnerable children living in poverty. Goddard was clear that the nonprofit needed more than just a new name, and she initiated a process to rebrand the organization. She started by engaging internal stakeholders in a strategy process to redefine the mission and values of the organization; this strategy work was closely connected to a branding process. The result of their effort included a new name and a new understanding of the brand and its core intent. Previously, the nonprofit had seen itself as a sponsorship organization. Its new strategy clarified that the purpose of the organization is to improve the lives of children, with the outcome for the child being the ultimate output of the organization's work. Linking the work on the strategy to the brand helped the organization develop a new brand identity that resonated with, and has been embraced by, the staff.

Sara Stuart, director of development and communication at Union Settlement Association, noted that her organization is in the midst of a long-term strategic planning process that includes branding. As part of this process, they have simplified the nonprofit's mission and clarified its brand identity. Stuart believes that by combining the branding and strategy work, the organization will be stronger and well positioned for the future.

Connecting work on the brand to work on an organization's strategy means that decisions about the brand are not made solely within the confines of communications and marketing departments, but must involve the organization's leadership, board, and executive team. As Noah Manduke concluded, "Brand strategy needs to be an enterprise-wide initiative. Nonprofits that rely on public support tend to do brand strategy from the marketing department. Ultimately brand is about 'being yourself on purpose,' and that purpose has to come from the strategic management of the organization." We believe that as organizations move toward viewing their brand as a strategic asset, rebranding efforts will be more closely tied to strategic planning efforts.

ALIGNING IDENTITY WITH MISSION

The Role of Brand Cycle places the brand within the larger context of not only organizational strategy but also the organizational mission and values. Some organizations align the brand identity more closely with the mission; others align it with more emphasis on their values. The relative emphasis of mission and values depends on the nature of the organization, but both are important. We will focus first on alignment of identity with mission.

Some organizations are building great brands without an explicit process to do so. They are sharply focused on their mission, and the internal brand identity emerges organically from this focus. They are doing good branding, perhaps without even realizing it. Dr. R. Balasubramaniam, founder of the Swami Vivekananda Youth Movement, described how his focus on the mission was central to the brand. "I didn't realize I was building a brand," he explained. "It's not something that happened by design because I was so focused on the mission. Focusing on the mission itself became brand building."

Some organizations may need a process to realign their brand so that it authentically reflects their existing mission. At Special Olympics, feedback received as the organization was ratifying a strategic plan made it clear that there was confusion among internal constituents about how to talk about the organization. Kirsten Suto Seckler, vice president of branding and communications, defined the issue: "Are we sports? Are we health? We didn't know how to talk about ourselves." After experiencing significant organizational growth, local programs and clubs had varying interpretations of the Special Olympics brand. The organization recognized the need to realign the brand to clarify who it was, what it does, and why it matters. Seckler described the process: "We made it clear we weren't rebranding, but trying to synthesize all the things we do in a simpler way." A steering committee started by conducting an audit, collecting many of the visual representations, messages, and brand materials from across the organization and soliciting broad input. The committee worked hard to define and develop a guiding idea for the organization that is communicated in both words and pictures—an important attribute, given that the organization works in more than 170 countries and with populations that don't always have strong literacy skills. Historically, Special Olympics spent a lot of time focusing on the first part of its mission: sports training and athletic competition. The realignment work, however, led to a guiding idea and brand model that is about more than just the athlete and conveys the concept of "revealing the champion in all of us." This new brand model is aligned with the entire mission, as well as with the organization's vision and values, and explains more of the reason *why* the organization exists. "With the results of this effort, we have seen massive alignment. People are so excited about the work, and we've seen so much adoption," explained Seckler. Aligning the brand with the mission has created more internal clarity and greater consistency throughout the organization. People have a common understanding of the brand and common tools (templates and guidelines) that they can use to support communications.

Other organizations achieve alignment by redefining their mission and brand identity simultaneously. When she joined Barakat, Angha Childress, executive director, recognized the need to rebrand, including the need to clarify the mission, the identity, and the connection between the two. "The previous mission statement was too broad, and the logo made no sense," she recalled. "I set out to change that." Childress began the rebranding by working with the board, facilitating a process that allowed constituents to reflect on the organization's past and confirm its vision for the future. "Branding occurred during and through this process of really deep thought and discussion, which involved all the stakeholders, including our two biggest funders." Childress used the organization's history and roots, as well as data from the field, to help the board and staff hone the new brand identity and rewrite the mission. The mission and vision statements describe the belief in the fundamental human right to education, which is central to the brand identity. "What strengthens our brand is seeing the belief, passion, and dedication that people have for the mission—that alone speaks volumes about the brand. In [the teachers'] mind it's the brand that matters to them, this agency that they are helping create because they are investing in their community."

In some cases, the work on brand identity can be a catalyst for reviewing and changing the organizational mission. Kali Baker, director of communications for the Omaha Community Foundation, discussed how the foundation's mission changed as a deeper understanding of the brand identity evolved during its recent rebranding process. "The old mission was about the organization's service to donors," Baker explained. "By adding words about the community and nonprofits, the new mission better articulates who we are and what we do." It is interesting to note that the old mission reflects the old brand paradigm of brand as a fundraising tool focused on the donor, whereas the new mission includes beneficiaries and partners, making the new brand more strategic and reflective of the organization's operations. The organization attributes much of its recent growth to the work it has done on its brand. From 2006 to 2011, assets grew 54 percent, and new gifts grew 221 percent.

For the majority of organizations we talked with, the brand is the reflection and embodiment of the mission. For some organizations, however, even though the mission plays an important role in brand identity, the organization's values may play an even more important one.

ALIGNING IDENTITY WITH VALUES

For organizations that have a broad mission and a wide variety of programs and initiatives, aligning the identity with the mission can be challenging. We believe that these types of organizations may have an easier time achieving brand Integrity by focusing on alignment of identity with the organization's values. Values can provide a unifying theme that cuts across programs and appeals to multiple audiences.

The management of BRAC, a large international development organization, recognized that as the organization grew, new employees no longer fully understood the organization's core values. Social enterprises, focused on increasing product sales, were at times working at cross-purposes with the values of the organization's development pro-grams. Brand Integrity was a real challenge. "We needed to get to the core of what we do best and how we do it," said Asif Saleh, senior director of strategy, communications, and capacity. "How do we make our people understand the social nature of the brand? How do we run all our efforts with the brand identity in mind?" he asked. The rebrand-ing work that BRAC undertook looked at the organization's work and theory of change and included input from internal stakeholders as well as an external brand perception survey. The organization worked hard to distill the principles that guided its work down to four core values that are at the heart of the BRAC brand. As a large, diverse organization, anchoring the brand in these four values helps provide consistency across the organization. The organization is now working on internal communications and training, using stories to convey the essence of its brand.

Foundations typically reflect the values of their founder, and it is thus not surprising that they relate their brands closely with their values. The Ford Foundation views the connection of values and brand as criti-cal. Marta Tellado explained, "Values and mission are the bedrock of the brand. In order for the brand to be credible and effective, it really needs to reflect those values. The brand can be an effective tool in helping us maintain our discipline around how we communicate our mission and values."

At the Gates Foundation, the values of optimism, collaboration, rigor, and innovation have been in place since the beginning of the organization. "The values are primarily meant for how we conduct ourselves," said Tom Scott, "but they also relate to partnerships and interactions with other audiences." He added, "I believe that your orga-nization's core values really are your brand. If you are living your core values and people believe them and exhibit them, then that will be the external manifestation of your brand. You can't have one set of values internally and then try to communicate a different set externally. If you have a stated set of values and you're not living up to those values, guess what? That's your brand too."

This idea of living the values is connected to how authentic an organization and its brand are perceived to be. All aspects of Buy42's brand and business model, from its hiring practices to its communica-tions and advocacy strategy, are based on the core value of taking action in a purposeful way to benefit others as well as oneself. Buy42 is a Chinese organization that takes donations of unwanted clothes, sorts and photographs them with support from disabled staff, resells items online, and uses 50 percent of the proceeds to support projects to help the disabled. The Buy42 brand means that a single action (buying clothes or cleaning out your closet) can benefit two people (yourself and someone else). This is directly tied to the underlying values of the organization, which emphasize that everything can be done not only to satisfy one's own needs but also to help others. Xian Zhou, founder and CEO, described this further: "We provide a three-in-one solution for reducing carbon emissions, charity fundraising, and creating job opportunities for the disabled. The brand has to explain this entire value proposition and overcome resistance to charities in general and second-hand clothing in particular."

In our experience, organizational values tend to remain relatively stable over time, providing an important anchor for the brand. Values are critical to brand: they shape brand identity, and those organizations that "live" their values are more likely to be perceived as authentic brands; their brand image aligned with their brand identity. It is to a discussion of brand image that we now turn.

BRAND IMAGE

Brand image is the external perception of the organization held by the organization's various stakeholders. We notice that some people confuse the external image and the internal identity, but these are two different concepts. The brand image is a psychological construct held in the minds of external audiences and so does not truly belong to the organization itself. As we have seen in previous chapters, the brand image also reflects the differentiation and positioning of the brand.

A strong brand image often combines an instantly recognizable visual image with a clear understanding of what the organization is, does, and stands for. However, a brand is much more than a logo and tagline. Brand image becomes powerful and distinctive only when the visual aspects of the brand are connected in the minds of key audiences with a deeper understanding of the organization itself. As Jenny Waggoner, president of the League of Women Voters of California, noted, "For generations, our concept of brand was largely print based, a very top-down, traditionalist view. Today we need to know more about our audiences' brand experience. Not just logos and colors, but how they feel about us."

When people equate brand image with just the visual aspects of the brand—a logo and tagline—it can create a lot of trouble. The logo and tagline, which are often great points of contention and consternation during any rebranding work, are less important than articulating an underlying understanding of the organization. This is why it is critical to spend time internally explaining and communicating that the visual aspects of the brand are simply the expression or representation of the brand identity. As such, the visual identity should also embody the strategy, mission, and values of the organization. YMCA Canada spent a lot of time on education and training regarding their brand, but did not radically change the logo or spend money on professional signage. "We really wanted the discussions and branding work *not* to focus on the logo," said Meghan Reddick. "We wanted to demonstrate that brand is so much more than just a logo, more than just what you look like and what you say. It's also about what you *do*. Many organizations fail when they focus on the logo and forget about the rest of what brand is all about."

Kate Roberts, vice president of corporate marketing, communications and advocacy at PSI, agreed that the organization's work and people are more important than a logo in conveying a brand. "It's not about a logo or brand colors," she explained. "It's about the work. It's not about having a fancy brand manual—it's about building your brand from within with the people that you hire. It is our work that builds our brand."

As Roberts emphasized, brand image is not simply the result of communications emanating from the organization. As we will see in the chapter on brand Democracy, communications, largely due to the rise in social media, are no longer simply a one-way download of information but instead a complex web of interactions and feedback. Brand audiences are obtaining and exchanging information about an organization and developing a brand image based both on what the organization is saying and on what other sources are saying about that organization. External audiences are increasingly relying on information that comes from their own experience or from other individuals via social networks rather than from the organization directly.

An organization's brand image is shaped by the multiple touchpoints that brand audiences have with that organization, from the time they first hear about an organization to how and when they engage with it and decide to support it. Here, brand ambassadors, both internal and external to the organization, play a critical role in influencing brand image through what Novy-Hildesley called "honest signals"—actions and experiences speaking louder than words. As we will see in the discussion of brand Affinity, openly sharing brand materials and tools with a variety of partners can really help extend an organization's reach and access to brand touchpoints.

The brand's external image is experienced by audiences through every interaction with the organization. As Peter Duffin, vice president of brand and marketing at the Lincoln Center for the Performing Arts, noted, "When we think about the brand, we really look at it from the perspective of the patrons and other audiences, such as artists and trustees. We think about all the touchpoints these audience members have with us. All of these connections are opportunities for us to brand the relationship with our patrons along the entire arc of their engagement with Lincoln Center."

Organizations, particularly if they are still somewhat in the old brand paradigm, can sometimes focus too much on their external image, spending time and resources to build and control images in an effort to raise visibility. Mihela Hladin, founder and CEO of Greenovate, explained that this may increasingly be a waste of resources. "In China," she explained, "the environment is changing so fast that it becomes less about what you say and more about what you actually do."

ADDRESSING MULTIPLE AUDIENCES

Part of the complexity of building a brand in the nonprofit sector is the diversity and breadth of the external audiences that a single brand must address. These can include beneficiaries, donors, staff, volunteers, partners, supporters, and the public. For many nonprofit managers, having to address multiple audiences is often viewed as a dilemma or an unreasonable demand to place on a single brand. But when organizations create different brand identities for different audiences, the result can be confusing and can lead to a fundamental misunderstanding of the organization itself.

Many managers admit to emphasizing different aspects of their brand with different audiences. Christine Letts at the Harvard Kennedy School noted that often there are tensions inherent in communicating a consistent organizational identity and brand and addressing different audiences. "I think that nonprofits are sometimes a little schizophrenic when it comes to what they think different audiences will respond to. When they are with beneficiaries, they want to be humble and serving. When they are with donors, they need to be competent. So they walk this fine line about touting themselves and projecting the right image."

Shimmy Mehta, founder and CEO of Angelwish, a nonprofit that provides psychosocial and educational support through gift giving for children and adolescents living with chronic illnesses, described the tension around managing brand across multiple audiences: "Initially, brand didn't play much of a role for us. We picked the name Angelwish because it was a good fit that sounded good and that we could grow with. But the brand took on different meanings based on who the audience was." Explained Mehta, "While the innocent kids were sometimes thought of as the angels, there were times the donors were the angels."

Nonprofits must understand all of their audiences' needs and strive to find commonality, based on the mission and values, that resonates with these multiple audiences. We believe that these organizations should use brand Democracy to create a single, well-defined brand identity for the organization as a whole. Flexibility at the local level can be accomplished if the organization first achieves brand Integrity. Projecting different brand images, whether intentionally or accidentally, is a mistake. A clearly focused and differentiated brand should be based on mission and values and a single value proposition. Consistency across different brand audiences, as we have previously noted, is one of the drivers of brand equity and what makes a strong brand. Focusing on beliefs, in the form of mission or values, not only appeals to a range of audiences but also is more authentic. Novy-Hildesley calls this "finding your voice."

We agree with Steve Davis, president and CEO of PATH, who believes that "brand Integrity is a particular challenge for large NGOs with project-based funding. Perceptions of the organization depend on which piece of the elephant you experience." But as we all know, just because brand Integrity is difficult to achieve, doesn't mean you shouldn't strive toward it. Focusing on horizontal competencies and values can help an organization find a unifying theme that cuts across diverse projects and initiatives. Communicating the brand across different audiences became easier for the staff at the Ford Foundation, for example, after taking a hard look at whom they were trying to reach As Marta Tellado described, "There is something that unifies all of our audiences. Our work is about social change, so the unifying element is that our audiences, such as grantees, public officials, and policy think tanks, are social change makers. Having clarity about that has been really helpful for us." Finding the unifying themes and striving for a consistent brand image for the organization are critical to achieving brand Integrity and creating cohesion and trust.

ALIGNING BRAND IDENTITY AND BRAND IMAGE

A nonprofit brand is most powerful and develops the greatest equity when the organization's internal brand identity and external brand image are aligned with each other and with its values and mission. We refer to this alignment as brand Integrity. Brand Integrity is typically achieved and maintained through an iterative process, which ensures that the external perceptions match the internal understanding of the brand. As Will Novy-Hildesley described, "When effectively executed, brand is the exquisite bridge between program strategy and external communications. Don't think you can do great branding or communications work without a sound strategy . . . Everything you see in communications is symptomatic of strategic issues. And those are brand strategy issues."

Indeed, it is often a misalignment between internal identity and external image that drives rebranding efforts in many nonprofit organizations. The result of alignment in mission, values, brand image, and brand identity is strong brand Integrity. It is this brand Integrity that helps build cohesion internally and drives trust between the nonprofit and its partners, beneficiaries, participants, and donors.

When PSI, an organization devoted to improving the health of poor and vulnerable people in the developing world, conducted an organizational brand audit, they found a mismatch between external perceptions and their internal identity. Kate Roberts explained, "We were seen as lone rangers, which surprised us. We were also perceived as expensive, which is not the case—we are actually one of the most cost-effective organizations in the sector. But because we were efficient and speedy, there was the sense that we were expensive." These two areas of external misperception were subsequently the basis for two of the organization's four brand pillars—strong partnerships, speed and efficiency, scale and measurement, and lasting solutions.

Alignment between identity and image starts with defining brand identity and then developing an approach that repositions this identity with respect to the existing brand image. Adam Hicks, former VP of marketing and communications for CARE USA, reflected on how Helene Gayle, president and CEO, initiated internal conversations on how to reposition CARE's brand. "Helene Gayle pushed [CARE USA's] programming leadership to answer the question, what is CARE's unique theory of change? One aspect that emerged from this reflection was that marginalized girls and women were at the center of all of our programming. And so that is what we centered on in terms of our positioning." Hicks believes that this repositioning has resulted in better brand Integrity—the organization's work, mission, and image are all in alignment.

In other cases, alignment between identity and image emerges from a deeper understanding of the perceptions of key audiences. We discussed in Chapter Three how the Center for Civilians in Conflict's rebranding effort incorporated input from external stakeholders to realign the identity and image. For Sarah Holewinski, the rebranding effort has yielded much more than a new name and logo. The alignment of identity and image can be seen directly in the changes the nonprofit has made. In recognition of their identity as a policy organization, they have redesigned their website to reflect a more professional, policy-oriented approach, using photos that reflect their human rights values. They have also refocused their fundraising, identifying supporters who are interested in their systems and policy approach and moving away from direct mail campaigns. Holewinski described how the process led to a recognition that they are really about "working with people who have the power to transform the planning, conduct, and aftermath of conflicts for civilians—from military officials and policymakers to UN bodies and civilians themselves. The study [on external image] fed into our mission and helped define and understand our audiences and partners. We are now much more confident in terms of who we are and who we are not," explained Holewinski, "and this gives us great focus and validates our internal brand identity. I used to struggle to explain what we do, but now I have phenomenal clarity, and I love knowing who we really are."

Rebranding initiatives are often begun by organizations whose activities have evolved from their initial focus such that the brand identity, including what the organization actually does, has changed to the extent that it is no longer aligned with the external brand image held in the minds of its multiple brand audiences. This lack of alignment between identity and image can cause confusion and weaken the brand's equity. As Peter Bell noted from his CARE experience, "Closing the gap between CARE's internal sense of organizational identity and its practices in external communications" was central to feeling that CARE was branding "with integrity."

The objective of aligning brand identity and image is to reach a fundamental understanding of the who, what, and why of the organization. As Wilmot Allen, nonprofit adviser and founder of the Partnership for Urban Innovation, described, including external constituents is key in bridging the gap between internal and external stakeholder perceptions and sharing ownership of the brand to build "empathy with their constituency." This alignment, built by engaging various audiences, ultimately supports an organization's ability to achieve mission impact. Meghan Reddick at YMCA Canada explained her experience: "We needed to get some clarity in our image and align what we do with how we are perceived. We felt that in order to deliver quality service and serve our mission, we needed to focus on what we stand for and what's our cause."

The process of alignment, discussed further in Chapter Eight, is an ongoing one, not a one-time event. Alignment means that the organization is truly doing what it says it is doing. We believe that this aspect of brand Integrity can serve as a type of accountability mechanism for your organization. Bringing in the voices of external audiences is important to informing the internal understanding of identity and enabling this alignment to occur. Perceptions can change over time, as can the organizational culture, mission, and strategy. Ongoing dialogue is therefore necessary to maintain brand Integrity.

USING BRAND INTEGRITY TO SUPPORT DECISION MAKING

We talked to many people who explained how brand Integrity helped them with decision making, in terms of both programs and communications. When the brand is connected to and a reflection of the organization's strategy, mission, and values, it can become a filter for decision making, enabling the organization to deploy the brand with integrity.

At Humanity United, Mike Boyer, vice president of strategic communications, described brand as "the north star internally for the entire organization." Humanity United is one of several independent foundations created by the Omidyar Group. "Our brand doesn't just provide our staff with a sense of identity, but it also places our work within the context of the broader Omidyar Group of philanthropic organizations." As is true for many large organizations that have a broad mission, it is the values, and their integration within the brand, that provide a unifying theme, in this case connecting independent but related foundations.

This concept of the brand as the north star, or as Steve Davis at PATH put it, "the white lines on the road," also suggests that the brand can help keep the organization focused and protect against mission drift. Peter Walker of the Feinstein International Center at Tufts University remarked that strong brands draw boundaries around what sorts of work and alliances should be taken on. "The brand allows you to know what the limits are . . . It's almost like mission statement plus. If I go beyond this, I go beyond the brand, and I'm distorting it."

We heard from some of our interviewees that their brand helped clarify what initiatives fit with their mission and what needed to be realigned. As Anne Goddard at Childfund explained, the rebranding "allowed us to determine whether the 'side dishes' in our grant portfolio should have a home. Once we defined our strategy and brand, including our core outcomes and how we work, we understood where these pieces fit. Some programs had migrated in terms of their focus. They were good programs, but they no longer fit with the brand."

Brand Integrity can also help an organization identify what programs are needed to implement the mission. Goddard described how she observed this during the recent rebranding effort. Staff were encouraged to think in a creative way about what it meant to live the brand, putting the child's experience at the center of their work. As a result, they developed new ideas for programs that reflect the organization's values and support the mission and brand.

We also heard how the brand can help organizations deploy or communicate their brands with integrity when issues arise that challenge an organization's core beliefs or values. This can include decisions about who to accept as donors, who might speak on behalf of the organization, how to respond to a variety of ethical issues, and what images to use in communications. When the brand reflects the organization's core values, potential conflicts or issues that might stretch the brand are easier to recognize. Should an organization accept funds from a partner or company that may be contributing to the social problems that the organization is working to change? Should an organization expand into an area that is outside its core mission in order to help a partner? These may still be challenging decisions, but the brand helps raise or frame the question. Using the brand as a compass can bring attention to potential conflicts in a way that puts the mission and values at the center of the issue.

Amnesty International's recent rebranding effort captured the core values of the organization in the Little Yellow Book, a guide for implementing the organization's brand. These values are not just abstract; they are an integral part of the brand that helps in day-to-day decision making. For example, Amnesty staff developed a Facebook-like website called Tyrannybook, where individuals could create and comment on profiles of tyrants. Another initiative led to the creation of an app called Bulletproof, which depicted a prisoner being dragged to a firing squad. The object of the game was to stop the bullets from the firing squad in order to save the prisoner. The brand and work that had been done on the organization's global identity helped Amnesty consider whether these initiatives were a fit or not. They were appealing to new audiences, but the issue was whether or not they fit with the organization's values. Ultimately, Tyrannybook was taken down, and Bulletproof survived (Stone, 2011, p. 6).

At Acumen Fund, the idea of "seeing a world beyond poverty" has helped guide decisions on what photographs to use on its website and in print materials. Yasmina Zaidman discussed how rather than motivating donors by showing pitiful photographs, the fund chooses images of "pride and dignity" rather than ones that "dehumanize the people whom we want to actually help."

The values articulated through the brand work at Save the Redwoods League have also helped guide the nonprofit's decision making. When news emerged that the California State Parks had not reported funds that might have been used to prevent potential park closures, many individuals were outraged. Jennifer Benito-Kowalski explained, "Some of our members were angry with the State Parks situation, but we wanted to stay positive. Our brand is about bringing people together, figuring out how to move forward, partnering with like-minded individuals or organizations, and working toward solutions that ultimately protect the redwoods." The brand was integral to keeping them focused on the right message, staying positive, and confirming the need to continue to work together. "We have to be positive and look at that bigger vision because we are here for the redwoods."

Similarly, when there have been issues that affect redwood groves, their brand has helped guide their response. When the California Department of Transportation (Caltrans) proposed a highway project that would affect redwoods in Richardson Grove, stakeholders wanted Save the Redwoods League to be a vocal opponent of the project, instead of staying on the sidelines. "We didn't advocate for either side," Benito-Kowalski explained. "We are the group that brings people together. We were challenged and criticized, but we stayed true to who we are and made the best decision for us."

Not only does brand Integrity create strong brands that contribute to organizational cohesion and trust, but a clear and focused brand with high brand Integrity can help staff with decision making at many levels. When the brand reflects the organization's strategy, mission, and values, then decisions regarding resource allocation, programs, and partnerships can be made more efficiently. Achieving or striving for brand Integrity is not without its challenges, however, as we shall see in the next section.

CHALLENGES OF INTEGRITY

Brand Integrity is dynamic. As external contexts change and internal capacities evolve, nonprofits must adapt in order to maintain alignment. Although organizational values may not change much over time, programs, brand identity and brand image, and even the mission do change. Our interviewees highlighted a number of challenges in aligning brand identity and brand image. These include addressing the tendency for image to lag identity, balancing responsiveness with mission focus, and resisting the allure of fame and visibility.

Addressing the Tendency for Image to Lag Identity

When an organization changes its brand identity, alignment with the image takes time. This is particularly true for those organizations that have been in operation for a long time and whose programming has evolved significantly over that time. External stakeholders often hold on to the brand image they initially developed when first encountering the nonprofit. Although brand identity may have kept up more closely with an evolving mission and programmatic focus, the perceptions held in the minds of the external audiences may remain anchored in the past. Organizations need to recognize that this lag may exist, and leadership and staff should not be disheartened when early assessments do not demonstrate alignment—change takes time. Addressing the misalignment that results from a tendency for image to lag identity presents an opportunity to engage external stakeholders in discussion and work toward brand Integrity.

Balancing Responsiveness with Mission Focus

We have suggested that it is important to listen to target audience needs and respond to market changes. At the same time, we encourage organizations to know themselves and stay focused on their mission and values. This can sometimes lead to a difficult balancing act. As Jeb Gutelius, a freelance nonprofit adviser, suggested, "Donors like to be listened to, but also want to know that the organization has its own compass." There is a tension and balance between listening to other audiences and staying true to oneself. We recognize that this tension exists and that each organization must acknowledge it and take it into account as they manage the dynamic alignment between brand identity and image.

Resisting the Allure of Fame and Visibility

Some organizations can become "addicted" to fame and visibility in their quest to establish a strong brand image. If the brand work becomes more about generating visibility, recognition, and fame, and less about implementing the mission or achieving brand Integrity, the risk is that audiences will start to lose trust. Jack Sim (aka Mr. Toilet), founder and CEO of the World Toilet Organization, described the risk organizations face when they focus too much on promoting themselves rather than the issue: "Organizations can get addicted to fame and visibility, and it becomes all about them rather than about the cause or mission. That's why we get brand names taped into donated latrines. The quest for visibility does not necessarily further the mission." When the focus of this effort to increase visibility is driven by the old fundraising paradigm, it may be to the detriment of the cause and overall impact. An emphasis on the organization's brand and visibility might not only crowd out partner brands but also have negative repercussions on the way the organization is perceived by different external stakeholders.

SUMMARY

Aligning the identity with the mission, values, and strategy creates internal cohesion—that is, internal audiences fully understand the who, what, and why of the organization. Achieving alignment between the internal identity and the external image requires input from various audiences. This alignment contributes to external trust and ultimately to greater mission impact, as described in the previous chapter on the Role of Brand Cycle. Martin Lloyd, marketing communications manager, described how Greenpeace was trusted in Argentina: "People understood that we were committed to what we believe in, or that we could not be corrupted, we couldn't be bought off. I know we stood up for what we believed in, and in a society which was having issues with corruption and lack of rule of law, being willing to do that kind of thing makes you a lot of friends. It also makes some powerful enemies, but it makes you an awful lot of friends. And that in turn enabled us to generate huge amounts of popular pressure and to secure some really big victories in terms of defending the forest."

Integrity is a state of being, in which the brand identity and image are consistent across audiences, both internal and external. This consistency and alignment support improved decision making, where the brand helps frame issues and choices for individuals and the organization. A strong brand becomes an accountability mechanism, ensuring that what the organization is saying and doing are one and the same. As Anne Goddard stated, "Our rebranding was all about building integrity and aligning our mission and brand and core values. We worked hard on integrity. What you see is what you get." Brand Integrity is achieved through the process of brand Democracy, described in the following chapter.

CHAPTER

6

BRAND DEMOCRACY

Brand Democracy refers to the extent to which an organization engages its board, staff, members, participants, volunteers, supporters, and other stakeholders in both defining and communicating the brand identity. Brand Democracy is an approach through which an organization can achieve brand Integrity. It has three components. The first is the participative process used to define the brand identity. The second component reflects a change in mindset whereby the organization views stakeholders, both internal and external, as the brand's ambassadors and advocates. It also takes into account changes in communications, which are evolving from a one-way broadcast to a process of authentic interactive engagement. The third component reflects a shift from the control and policing of an organization's brand to a more democratic style of organizational communication that relies on guidelines, tools, and templates and allows for flexibility within defined parameters.

Brand Democracy and brand Integrity are closely intertwined. A participative process helps create brand Integrity by engaging internal and external stakeholders to define brand identity. At the same time, the outcome of brand Integrity helps enable an organization to empower brand ambassadors and emphasize brand guidance rather than brand control. Brand Integrity helps ensure that the brand remains strong and is not diluted or hijacked in the process of brand Democracy. When the brand is focused, clear, and well understood by all, leadership finds it both easier and more desirable to encourage greater individual expression of the brand. This clarity also makes it easier to relax the notion of strict brand control and allows the organization to provide guidance and principles for brand management instead. The key is to align the brand with the mission and values of the organization such that all communications are in service to this mission and these values.

It is clear that the explosion in social media is increasingly driving the need for brand Democracy. Communications are taking place beyond the reach of the organization, among and between a myriad of stakeholders, rather than just between the organization and its audiences. The public is communicating an organization's brand whether they've been deputized or not. Implementing brand Democracy reflects the shift to the new brand paradigm and helps an organization harness the strength of social media. It also recognizes that the old model of strict brand control is no longer feasible.

IMPLEMENTING A PARTICIPATIVE PROCESS

At the heart of the concept of brand Democracy is the notion of broad participation in defining and communicating the brand identity. Brand Democracy engages stakeholders in discussions around brand identity, which results in a clearer, shared internal perception of the brand, which is then articulated and communicated in a way that is both consistent and authentic. This process of participative engagement not only gets everyone on the same page with regard to the brand identity, but also creates brand ambassadors within and beyond the organization and results in cohesion throughout sometimes large and dispersed organizations.

Supporters, donors, corporations, government representatives, foundations, and staff were all involved in revising Childfund's core intent, mission, outcomes, values, and brand. Anne Goddard expressed surprise at how well the new brand and strategy were received and how positive the results were. She attributes this to the participatory and integrated approach used by the organization. Barakat also solicited broad input during its rebranding, and Angha Childress explained that rebranding was "a learning process which involved all the internal stakeholders and outside donors and by which everyone discussed and learned what Barakat really is: who we are and what we do."

For Lincoln Center for the Performing Arts in New York City, a redesign of the physical environment informed its rebranding process. Changes to its physical space had the goal of opening the campus up—

in essence, encouraging greater participation. Peter Duffin explained, "We wanted to open up the campus, integrating the life of the arts center into the life of the community." This sense of openness was integrated into the organization's rebranding process and ultimately into its new brand too.

Participation of stakeholders is critical to understanding the various brand audiences and finding the connections between them. Without real data, whether in the form of focus groups, online surveys, or more rigorous analyses, perceptions about the brand are based on assumptions. Data can help bring some objectivity to this process and ground the brand in reality. Collecting data on the perceptions of key external audiences is critical to aligning identity and image and reshaping the brand.

Networks and affiliated organizations can also use participative approaches to brand management, although doing so may require more time to implement. These entities need to incorporate brand Democracy both horizontally across affiliates and vertically within the organization. Social Venture Partners is a network of thirty autonomous organizations, each with a dual mission to strengthen nonprofits by investing in and engaging in their work and to educate its partners about their role in philanthropy. The network collaborated to develop a joint sense of organizational personality and identity. "The process was extensive," explained Elizabeth Benedict, communications director. "We knew it was going to take time and involve many people. Our work was to find the essence of who we are and talk about our purpose and passion through our own stories."

Although it does take time for any organization to implement a participative process, we believe that the benefits are derived as much from the process itself as from the end product. Participation and engagement are at the heart of brand Democracy and help organizations build internal cohesion and a more representative and authentic brand identity. Benedict said that in her experience, "It's really about achieving buy-in. We wanted network representation, so we pulled together a brand liaison team and brand task force that included people from across the network, to build trust as well as support both for the process and the outcome. Part of the process is about building connections and listening to people. It takes time to do this properly!"

Building consensus was also an important part of the rebranding work undertaken by Oxfam America. When the staff worked on their brand, it was important that they gained "a deep understanding of the process by which you're creating the brand so that it's not back behind the curtain and then suddenly you roll it out. We are a consensus-driven organization," explained Rachel Hayes, senior director, communications and community engagement. "People need to feel that they've been informed along the way, that they've been consulted, that they have a role to play in expressing their points of view." This participation helped reinforce the culture and values of the organization, building trust internally and, ultimately, resulting in a stronger brand.

For Special Olympics, participation and engagement were critical to the success of the realignment effort. The organization formed a steering committee that represented the diversity of programs and stakeholders—athletes, volunteers, leadership, and regions—and followed an approach that was very democratic, transparent, and time limited. Kirsten Suto Seckler commented on the importance of considering the needs of the local coaches, parents, and volunteers: "One thing we learned throughout the process was that our brand lives and breathes at the very local level." By incorporating local input and broad representation from across the organization, their realignment process became a model for other organizational efforts. According to Seckler, "People are adopting [our] model of codevelopment because I think they saw how powerful it was for our brand work. If we actually engage our internal stakeholders in the work that we do, it is more powerful in the end."

Marta Tellado described the importance of broad participation at the Ford Foundation. "The process that we engaged in was one that involved the staff, grantees, and the board in genuine discussion and feedback. They can't sit outside the process of brand building; they must be part of it," she explained. "Their insights and participation are critical."

Brand Democracy does not mean that every stakeholder must have input or that the brand is subject to a vote. Senior management must shape the process and define how and when to solicit input. A few years ago, this was the task facing Marinke van Riet, international director of Publish What You Pay. Publish What You Pay is "a global network of civil society organizations united in their call for an open and accountable extractive sector, so that oil, gas, and mining revenues improve the lives of women, men, and youth in resource-rich countries." The coalition was formed in 2002 by 6 organizations, and in 10 years had grown to encompass 680 members in 59 countries. The organization recognized the need to reassess its mission and brand, and for van Riet, the key question was, "Does the brand still cover what we actually do?" The growth in the network meant that the organization no longer had a shared sense of brand identity. This was clear from internal and external assessments of how the organization was perceived by coalitions and partners as well as by current and former members. Van Riet used the brand IDEA framework to manage and guide the process of redesigning the organization's brand and strategy. Achieving brand Integrity necessitated a participatory approach that considered identity, image, strategy, and mission together. Given the diversity of the organization, broad participation was not easy to accomplish, but it was critical to building support and helping define the four strategic pillars of the organization and the shared brand identity. Branding became an integral part of strategic development, and as van Riet described, "The strategy development process has taken me from Almaty to N'Djamena, from Maputo to Dakar, from the U.S. to Norway, all with the view to be participatory and to promote ownership of the Vision 20/20." This vision describes the organization's strategy for 2012–2015 and outlines the organization's theory of change, operating principles, coalition standards, brand guidelines, and governance structure.

For some organizations, in-depth participation through a committee of stakeholders may be appropriate. For others, it may be more appropriate to have a smaller group work on rebranding and then invite feedback and comment. There needs to be consideration of how to keep the process efficient while engaging those who have something to contribute. The more inclusive and collaborative the discussions around brand, the greater the buy-in, but the longer the process can take.

It is important to reiterate that this process should involve both internal and external audiences. We are seeing more organizations incorporate input not just from donors but from beneficiaries in order to shape their brand identity. Extending participative engagement to beneficiaries will, we believe, result in even stronger brands. The Girl Effect, a movement created to promote support for the potential of adolescent girls to end poverty, actively engages supporters, partners, and beneficiaries. "When girls themselves are central actors in the design process," explained Maria Eitel, CEO and president of the Nike Foundation, "it also creates opportunities to develop connections between girls where they can share and collaborate with each other, ultimately working to solve problems themselves" (Kylander, 2011, p. 5).

EMPOWERING BRAND AMBASSADORS

The second component of brand Democracy concerns the decision to empower brand ambassadors. This is one of the most exciting outcomes of a brand Democracy approach. It reflects a new mindset for how the organization views both its stakeholders and its brand.

Brand Democracy is about encouraging participation in defining and communicating the brand, such that everyone becomes a brand ambassador. Brand Integrity is both a precursor to and outcome of empowering brand ambassadors. When internal stakeholders (staff and volunteers) understand the brand and share a belief in the mission and values conveyed by the brand, they find it easier to advocate authentically for the brand. The more clearly and authentically the brand identity is portrayed by these internal stakeholders, the more effective and consistent are the communications and resulting brand image.

Brand Democracy may start by engaging internal stakeholders, but needs to expand to include all audiences—volunteers, donors, beneficiaries, partners, and the public. As Tom Scott of the Gates Foundation said,

> You have to get it right internally because you will never get it right externally if you don't. Your employees are your brand ambassadors. You can think of it as concentric circles. Our employees are the closest to us, and we have to get our interactions with employees right, because they are the ones communicating with all the external audiences. Our next closest group is our partners, and those two audiences are fundamental in helping the external manifestation of your brand. You don't have two versions of your brand. Your brand is your brand, and you are stewards of it on a daily basis. The biggest challenge and opportunity going forward is really embedding the idea of our brand internally. We want to help people understand and give employees the right kind of tool kit and information to make better decisions about how to use the foundation voice and assets. I think that will lead to a more open brand.

Similarly, at the Ford Foundation, guidance is provided to staff, grantees, and other partners on effectively communicating Ford's mission and values. "We try to provide guidance through workshops and ongoing engagement with our staff across the globe. Our greatest asset is our people, and they serve as ambassadors for the foundation in our offices overseas," explained Marta Tellado. "We all have to take responsibility to communicate who we are and to clearly represent the mission of the foundation."

Embracing and internalizing the brand is the first step in encouraging people to be brand ambassadors. People who believe in the brand are going to share that belief through their work and through any interactions they have with others. Opportunity Fund encourages all employees to become brand ambassadors. "We have been building the idea that everyone is an ambassador for our brand," explained Caitlyn

McShane, marketing and communications director. One approach to achieving this is by asking internal stakeholders, "How can we find what's meaningful for you about our brand?" Finding the individual meaning helps ensure that the communication is authentic. Allowing flexibility in how people talk about the organization is an important component of brand Democracy. Opportunity Fund recognizes that everyone who works for the organization has a sphere of influence. Helping people talk about the organization in everyday situations can help spread the brand message.

Noah Manduke also spoke about the importance of empowerment, whereby "staff, supporters, and partners have a firm grasp of your unique significance and can advocate and evangelize" on behalf of the brand. This requires a continuous education process, according to Manduke. "Just because you say what you mean and do what you say doesn't mean that your staff or supporters will fully understand it." When staff and supporters believe and buy into the brand, then they are better able to communicate about the brand. Social Venture Partners also recognizes the value of empowerment. "It's important to have stories about people, not just organizations. It's better to empower people to think and live the brand and share their own stories in an authentic way," said Elizabeth Benedict.

The Public Education Foundation, in Chattanooga, Tennessee, demonstrates how brand Democracy can change the organizational culture. "We used to be very insular," said Christa Payne, vice president of external affairs. "Now we are totally out there. We are on NPR, we talk to journalists, we have elevator speeches and coffee mugs and pens, we developed collateral, we redesigned our website . . . All these marketing approaches that a few years ago we would never have done. But we did it all because of the buy-in. Now everyone feels like a brand ambassador."

When there is ongoing education and alignment of the brand and what it means, staff and the board can more readily internalize the brand and ultimately contribute to the organization by "living the brand" and becoming its most important ambassadors. As Holly Ross, former executive director of Nonprofit Technology Network, indicated, "Building brand with our staff and board has been essential to our success. Staff and board members are encouraged to define what about the brand they most relate to and use that as a basis for articulating the brand." Brand management in general and the empowerment of brand ambassadors in particular are continuous.

Internal and external stakeholders are both important audiences for the brand and important groups for communicating the brand. The Internet makes it much easier for individuals outside the organization to share their views, and people are increasingly relying on information (reviews and comments) shared by the public. Organizational boundaries are becoming more porous, and social media has made everyone a potential brand advocate. The result is increasing external participation in communicating the brand, making it difficult, if not impossible, to control brand communications. Alexis Ettinger, head of strategy and marketing at Skoll Centre for Social Entrepreneurship at Oxford University, expanded on this: "Between our website, our Twitter presence, our Facebook, and YouTube pages, it would be insane to try to control that footprint. So again, there are ways to keep consistency and continuity, but the masses will talk whether you like it or not." John Quelch of Harvard Business School also noted that "Organizations don't own their brands. Their brands are owned by the marketplace and audiences. What the audiences decide the brand is going to be is what it's going to be. So I think there will probably be a few NGOs that embrace this extremely effectively and understand the need to nurture their social communities. These organizations will end up doing extremely well." Jim Bildner of Harvard Kennedy School concurred and added that "brand ownership has shifted from the entity to the world."

Lincoln Center for the Performing Arts has recently experimented with social media and effectively created a new group of external brand ambassadors. "An interesting and successful use of social media was an experiment we conducted at a recent Paris Opera Ballet performance," explained Peter Duffin. "After the event, we posted photos of the performance on Facebook and shared them with the people who had attended the event. They shared them with their friends and showed them what they had missed—the reach and engagement from that simple and inexpensive approach was tremendous. It was a real win-win."

Lincoln Center recognizes that an ongoing dialogue with their key audiences will help keep their brand fresh.

> What we want to do now is to create a dialogue with our patrons, and we are searching for the best approaches and tools to engage people. When we launched the brand in February of this year, we asked people to share their best experiences and memories of Lincoln Center with us on our social channels. There were some wonderful posts; some people shared the time they attended a performance as a kid with their grandmother or the way some magical night influenced their lives. In fact, we opened a floodgate of transformative experiences, and it was reaffirmed that our patrons are passionate about this brand, which has a deep emotional connection and resonance for them.

Using social media has many merits, but requires authenticity. According to Tom Scott of the Gates Foundation,

> If it doesn't feel authentic or if it feels overly managed, the community gets that, and they smell that out pretty quickly. If you're just using social media as your own channel to put your own press releases out, you're probably not going to have engagement. The great thing about social media is it's so easy to measure. It's not about how many people "like" you, but you can do heat maps about where your conversations are taking place, how they spread, who's engaging. Social media is allowing us to measure and be responsive in ways that help us have even better conversations.

Social media can therefore become an important tool for implementing brand Democracy, particularly for engaging external brand ambassadors. It is also one of the drivers behind the shift from brand policing to brand guiding, as we describe in the following section.

USING GUIDING PRINCIPLES VERSUS STRICT CONTROLS

The concept of empowering brand ambassadors is closely tied with the idea of promoting the use of brand guidelines and principles rather than enforcing strict brand controls. This is the third component of brand Democracy. In the previous section, we discussed how this shift relates to the increasing role of social media, which makes strict brand control less feasible. Just as brand Integrity is necessary for empowering ambassadors, it is also necessary for this shift toward more guidance and less control. When the brand is aligned with the mission, values, and strategy, it provides clear parameters for how to talk about and use the brand. In the previous chapter on brand Integrity, we discussed the use of the brand in this way, where it serves as a guide for decision making, reducing the need for formal controls.

We came across many examples during our interviews which showed that when it comes to how their brand is communicated, organizations are focusing more on guidance through the development of templates and tools, and less on control. Laura Sanchez noted, "While I was at Living Cities, we realized that communications couldn't be tightly controlled anymore, so we put our focus into developing a guiding tone and voice and providing overarching guidance and tools that allowed people to take risks and experiment." The guidelines address the organization's brand communications via multiple mechanisms, including tweeting and blogging.

According to Elizabeth Benedict at Social Venture Partners (SVP), "In this day and age, you cannot be about control and having one single tagline or message. It's more about uncovering the essence of who you are and making space for people to be authentic. We are working toward a shared set of materials because it streamlines our work. Anytime I can make an SVP network staff member's or partner's job easier through a template or tool, it helps create buy-in and we have brand consistency."

At Girl Up, the teen advisory board and Girl Up clubs "are empowered to promote awareness about the issues and get the Girl Up brand out there," according to Alicia Bonner Ness, former development officer. Staff and champions are given talking points and guidelines, but "there is an element of permission built in. Champions are encouraged to own their own relationship with the brand identity and promote it to their network—it's not something that we try overly hard to micromanage."

Organizations that want both to speak with a single voice as a confederation and to allow for autonomous expression at the individual affiliate level need to balance these desires. Rachel Hayes at Oxfam America explained, "I describe the work we're doing in the global identity as creating bookends. These are the boundaries of our brand. And within those boundaries, each affiliate will have the ability to dial up and dial down certain messages to meet their local market, but they will be unified in overall look, in overall voice, in some graphic standards, and so on, so that we do convey one brand."

The use of guidelines, tools, templates, and principles in the management of the brand provides greater flexibility for regional or local offices or affiliates to adapt communications to their local environment. Brand management becomes more about monitoring and providing feedback and support for brand communications and less about policing and control. Expressing the brand as an idea and image instead of solely using words can also allow more flexibility for adapting the brand to local cultures or conditions.

Social media represents an avenue through which to explore this more democratic approach. Forward Greece, for example, has relied heavily on social media to reach a wider audience. At the same time, this has also allowed greater participation in shaping the direction of the organization. Panagiotis Vlachos, founder, explained, "Social media is a medium to mobilize people in order to increase your outreach. It's about giving people the opportunity to participate, modify political ideas and agendas, and through this participation to come closer and become part of the community." Interestingly, in this example, social media becomes a mechanism for the participative process as well as a tool for brand ambassadors.

Social media can also be a testing ground for new approaches. At Opportunity Fund, communications via social media have been a way to experiment with the brand and "lighten up our brand a little bit," according to Caitlyn McShane. Publications explain the programs and the impacts, but social media allows for more approachable messages. "These get greater traction than typical messaging—for example, tweeting, 'Just closed a loan to a bakery at Mission and 14th!'"

These approaches recognize that communications are increasingly two-way rather than one-way, which provides the opportunity for greater engagement by the audience. In this environment, it also becomes somewhat easier to measure the impact of various messages. Tools allow organizations to explore how conversations are spreading and what messages are generating a buzz and seem to be more relevant.

Maintaining cohesion across social media platforms is not always easy. "It was driving a lot of people crazy that when you went to Facebook, there wasn't just one place to get Special Olympics information, but there were thousands of pages," explained Kirsten Suto Seckler. "At the end of the day, what we realized is that we need to build a strategy around the fact that we have this great presence and we have this passion. Rather than trying to control that passion, let's give some guidance to that passion and let it live and breathe in a way that is positive for the entire organization." By embracing the connections that already existed, the organization is building brand ambassadors who are actively expressing excitement and pride in Special Olympics through social media. "We don't have a lot of marketing dollars. What we have [are] millions of people who love this organization. We are encouraging people to go out there and tell our story as well as their own."

Naturally, not all of what is expressed via social media is going to be positive for organizations, and the fear is that criticism can spread quickly. However, Ness at Girl Up found that negative social media comments did not have a big impact; even when discussions got heated among constituents online, there was little backlash. "You would have to be on the page when those comments are posted. It's not like sending out a huge press release." Overall, their experience has been positive. "We find that social media is high visibility for our target constituency and relatively low risk when it comes to negative perceptions." Other organizations have found that negative comments by critics on social media are quickly addressed by the organization's supporters and external ambassadors. This was the case for Free Lunch for Children; when an individual suggested online that there was some wrongdoing by the organization, supporters reacted quickly and strongly, countering the claim and demanding proof. The critical individual ended up admitting that he was mistaken and issuing an apology to the organization and its supporters. When an organization is operating with brand Integrity and brand Democracy, misstatements or misunderstandings that come up via social media are often resolved by external brand ambassadors (stakeholders and supporters), with less action required on the part of the organization.

CHALLENGES OF DEMOCRACY

Implementing brand Democracy is challenging, but we believe that the benefits of brand Democracy, both in terms of organizational cohesion and brand Integrity, substantially outweigh the costs in time and effort. Our interviewees expressed three main concerns: overcoming internal brand skepticism, avoiding brand anarchy, and gaining organizational support.

Overcoming Internal Brand Skepticism

Overcoming the brand skeptics within an organization is really the first (and potentially most difficult) task facing those driving the implementation of brand Democracy in a nonprofit. As we discussed in Chapter Four, brand skepticism is rooted in an outdated perception of the role of brand. Understanding the paradigm shift can help individuals overcome this initial skepticism. Internal branding, discussed in Chapter Three, can be used as an approach to both educate and engage skeptics in a discussion around brand, the role of brand, and brand identity. In our research, it was not unusual to find that some of the most engaged brand ambassadors were initially some of the organization's most vociferous brand skeptics.

Avoiding Brand Anarchy

Some people worry that brand Democracy will result in less consistency in external images and perceptions as everyone starts talking about the brand in his or her own way. Others are concerned that the broad participative process will not be able to result in a focused brand identity because many internal (and external) constituents have varying and sometimes conflicting views on the "who, what, and why." Special Olympics serves as a good example that dispels these concerns. In that case, realigning the brand reduced the amount of brand anarchy. As Kirsten Suto Seckler described, "Before the realignment, people were struggling. Every new idea got a new logo." Visual representations were not consistent, and there was confusion among internal stakeholders as to how to talk about the organization. By using a democratic process to achieve a single guiding idea behind the brand and creating simple templates and tools, Special Olympics has actually increased organizational clarity and consistency. For brand Democracy to work, the organization must have clarity in brand identity and work toward brand Integrity. Organizations that embrace brand Democracy but are not able to achieve a clear brand identity may struggle with brand anarchy. The recommendations and examples offered in Chapter Eight in regard to embracing participation and providing guidelines and tools should help manage this journey.

Gaining Organizational Support

It is essential to get the support and buy-in of the board and executive team in order to successfully implement brand Democracy. Sustained commitment from the top can help establish the culture necessary for a true participatory process. For organizations that hire new staff on a frequent basis, it can be difficult to identify new approaches to education and involvement that keep existing staff engaged. Some organizations worry that stakeholders will become tired and disengaged by yet another "brand meeting." Yet brand, as it is conceived of in the new paradigm, is part of everyone's job: it embodies the mission and helps the organization achieve impact. Internally, it can also be a great source of pride. Making brand part of every discussion and meeting rather than a separate issue to be worked on can be a natural and authentic way to keep everyone engaged. Organizational leaders can be key role models when they make brand part of their mindset.

SUMMARY

Brand Democracy is necessary to create brand Integrity, and brand Integrity helps in the implementation of brand Democracy. The two are closely intertwined. The participative process engages internal audiences and exposes them to data from external audiences; it goes beyond traditional internal branding efforts and creates organizational cohesion. As Noah Manduke explained, "If brand is where experiences happen, where work happens, it can't be something that sits back in corporate marketing . . . You can't disconnect it from the field. It has to be participatory from top to bottom from all functional areas."

Organizations that have brand Integrity can more easily empower their brand ambassadors, increasing the organization's capacity. Internal staff develop a stronger and more consistent understanding of the brand, which can improve their decision making. The participative process itself and the practice of providing guidance rather than strict control build organizational cohesion.

The Internet and social media in particular have widely expanded the potential pool of external brand ambassadors. The mindset of brand Democracy helps capitalize on this potential, recognizing that the paradigm of communications has changed. Although harnessing the power of social media can be difficult, there is real potential in mobilizing individuals and crowdsourcing, which can also lead to the identification of new and innovative ideas and greater participation.

Empowering brand ambassadors leads to greater trust externally. The cohesion and trust contribute to organizational capacity, whereby the organization can attract donors, partners, and human resources that are aligned with the brand and can contribute to increasing the organization's impact.

CHAPTER 7

BRAND AFFINITY

In this chapter, we describe the third concept of the brand IDEA framework, brand Affinity. We will examine both the drivers and characteristics of brand Affinity and touch briefly on the different types of partnerships, as well as what makes these brand partnerships successful. Brand Affinity refers to the way in which an organization extends its sphere of influence beyond the organization itself, in order to maximize social impact. Brand Affinity represents a mindset and an approach to brand management in which the focus is on shared social impact, rather than on individual internal organizational goals. An organization that demonstrates brand Affinity is one that recognizes and embraces the need to work with others to achieve its social objectives. It is also an organization that has brand Integrity, clearly defines its own brand identity and theory of change, and uses these to select and work with appropriate partners. By working with others and extending its brand to support partnerships, coalitions, or movements, an organization can maximize its collective social impact. Brand Affinity is about how to use brand to make these partnerships more effective in maximizing social impact.

The decision to use a brand Affinity approach to brand management is a proactive one. In some respects, brand Affinity is a continuation of the brand Democracy mindset, extending participation and access to the brand and brand assets beyond traditional organizational boundaries to include a variety of external partners. Brand Affinity is, however, a more complex and multifaceted concept, more context specific and fluid than either brand Integrity or brand Democracy. There is not one single brand Affinity approach; rather, brand Affinity may occur anywhere on a spectrum of engagement with other organizations, ranging from single partnerships to multiparty collaborations and movements. We believe that brand Affinity requires organizations to think about the impact that their brand can have beyond their own organization's work, in terms of broader collective influence and combined social impact. Brand Affinity requires trust and a willingness to be open and flexible and to establish cooperative relationships with others.

As we touched upon in the Introduction and first chapters of this book, brand Affinity bucks the traditional branding principles of competitive positioning and the use of the brand to build internal organizational capacity and drive financial results. Instead, it rests on the objective of driving toward a shared social goal. As Noah Manduke suggested, "the role of branding in the social sector is not to create competitive advantage; the role is to provide discipline in defining your unique contribution and value and how you are uniquely accelerating progress against these issues." We agree and would add that branding can also provide discipline in selecting and implementing partnerships.

THE DRIVERS OF BRAND AFFINITY

Just as the growth in social media and communications is a driving force behind brand Democracy, two factors support a brand Affinity approach: the partnership imperative and a focus on external social goals. We look at each of these in turn in this section.

The Partnership Imperative

Brand Affinity reflects the growth in partnerships, alliances, and collaborations of all kinds in the social sector. This phenomenon, according to Yankey and Willen (2010), stems from a growing realization that nonprofit organizations cannot achieve their social mission alone and that to maximize social impact, an organization must work with others. In addition, shifts in funding and turbulent economic times make collaboration more compelling, particularly as an increasing number of funders are explicitly requiring collaboration. Our interviewees confirmed that donors often prefer to fund collaborative efforts rather than individual organizations.

The necessity of partnerships is compellingly articulated by John Kania and Mark Kramer (2011) in their recent article "Collective Impact," in which they state, "In short, the nonprofit sector most frequently operates using an approach that we call isolated impact, oriented toward finding and funding a solution embodied within a single organization, combined with the hope that the most effective organizations will grow or replicate to extend their impact more widely." They add, however, that "despite the dominance of this approach, there is scant evidence that isolated initiatives are the best way to solve many social problems in today's complex and interdependent world. No single organization is responsible for any major social problem, nor can any single organization cure it" (p. 38).

Many of our interviewees echoed these sentiments. Li Ding, deputy director of Non-Profit Incubator (NPI) in China, stated that "nonprofits cannot succeed alone; to achieve their mission they must collaborate with many different players, including their own beneficiaries." Interestingly, the latter part of this statement also supports brand Democracy and the engagement of external stakeholders, and one can start to see how the concepts of brand Democracy and brand Affinity are related. Manduke suggested that "no one organization can do it alone. The biggest, hairiest issues in the world require a multisector, multipartner, multiplatform approach to creating system-level change." Although most nonprofit organizations are starting to understand that there is no one organization that is going to be able to solve the world's major social problems alone, few have taken the step to systematically use their brands to engage and promote partnerships. As Manduke concluded, "Being able to use your brand as a strategic asset in facilitating rather than eclipsing partnership is really important." As we have already discussed in Chapter Three, clarity in identity, theory of change, and differentiation and positioning are critical to determining which actors to partner with and how. Let us be clear here: our assumption is that collaboration results in greater impact. Brand Affinity is about how the brand can be used in support of these collaborations.

A Focus on External Social Goals

Many nonprofits reject the notion of competition and, as Oster (1995) notes, they have historically employed more collaborative than competitive approaches. If we move brand management beyond the traditional fundraising mindset, we can see more readily the utility and value of collaborating with others who share our goals. In our interviews, a striking number of nonprofit organizations affirmed their belief that they have no competitors, only collaborators.

All nonprofits have visions and missions that focus on goals and objectives that are societal in nature, rather than purely organization specific. In for-profit companies, the ultimate goals (typically financial) are specific and internal to that organization, and include revenue growth and increased profits and market share. In contrast, a nonprofit's ultimate goals (saving or improving people's lives, for example) are external to the organization, and their internal goals, usually revolving around capacity and resources, are simply means to an end, rather than the end or goal itself. Unlike for-profit entities, whose organizational goals are often tied to the organization's success relative to its competitors, non-profits focus on external goals whose attainment is possible only with the help of other organizations. Brand management in service of goal attainment is therefore fundamentally different in the two sectors. Unlike for-profits, nonprofits need to position their brands to further the common goals and, sometimes, gain support for a particular theory of change. This does not mean that nonprofits do not need to maintain brand differentiation and distinctiveness; indeed, as we argue, they may need these more. But it does mean that they can use their distinctive brands, based on a clear brand identity and theory of change, to understand which partners to work with and how to partner with other organizations to drive social impact.

CHARACTERISTICS OF BRAND AFFINITY

Brand Affinity comprises two sets of actions. First, armed with a clear understanding of the theory of change and brand identity, the organization identifies partners, reaches out, and uses brand to attract them. Second, brand Affinity includes using the brand to enhance the effectiveness of these partnerships in achieving mission and maximizing impact. Organizations with brand Affinity share space and credit generously, promote collective rather than individual interests, and use their brand as a magnet to draw partners and collaborators. By focusing on a greater shared goal, they are simultaneously achieving their own mission and helping others achieve theirs, resulting in greater overall impact. In some cases, this means promoting a partner's brand visibility over their own brand or lending credibility to partner brands by cobranding. In other cases, it means moving beyond the organization's own brand to jointly create a new brand that serves as an umbrella for a coalition or movement, under which many organizations can gather and work together toward the same goal. Building and managing brands with brand Affinity require a mindset in which the focus is on a shared or collective social mission and goal, and the approach includes open-source platforms, transparency, flexibility, and democracy.

Brand Affinity as a brand management approach and mindset can apply to the entire spectrum of partnerships, collaborations, networks, coalitions, and movements. The challenges and strategies may vary along this spectrum, but the fundamental approach of brand Affinity does not: identify and attract key partners with shared values and goals; use brand to manage and add value to those partnerships, using an open and flexible approach in sharing brand assets. Tom Scott described this shift in mindset, indicating that the Gates Foundation is exploring "a more purposeful approach to how we think about our brand. Not so much in the 'let's build our brand' way, but more 'what are the ways that we can use the brand to have the kind of impact we want to have?' " He defines his job as "managing the brand in a way to ensure we have enough flexibility to do what we need to do with our partners."

Identifying and Attracting Key Partners

Partnerships and cobranding efforts need to be built on a foundation of brand Integrity. The brand must be anchored in the strategy, mission, and values of the organization. Externally, brand image can be strengthened or weakened depending on whom you choose to partner with. As Will Novy-Hildesley said, "Who we partner with and how we cobrand defines our own brand." The first step in implementing brand Affinity is the same as for building brand Integrity: to clearly define and articulate one's own identity and values, as well as the theory of change espoused. The next step is to understand the other players in the ecosystem in order to assess potential partners. Mihela Hladin of Greenovate described this approach as follows: "We are very careful about who we choose to work with. The way we work, who we work with, and how we live our lives all have to be anchored in our values." In addition to fit with mission and values, a sound understanding of the organization's own identity and the unique role it plays within the theory of change will guide optimal partner selection. As Mallika Dutt, CEO of Breakthrough, put it, "We are becoming much more explicit about Breakthrough's methodology, about our approach, and not just about the issues we care about and our end goals, but being clear with ourselves and others about who we are and how we think, that this is our methodology, this is what we want to do. This enables us to approach our partners and say that is why we want your partnership." Finally, a keen understanding of differentiation and brand identity can, according to Sarah Holewinski at the Center for Civilians in Conflict, result in the development of new partners. "Now that we understand where we have the most impact," she explained, "we are taking ourselves out of a strictly traditional NGO role and striving to be the best at what we do well, and that means collaborating with nontraditional partners, such as former military advisers, social scientists, etc."

The Archive for Research in Archetypal Symbolism has started to recognize the need to work on its brand before reaching out to potential partners. The organization serves a wide variety of audiences, providing access to symbols and images through multiple mechanisms. Allison Tuzo, collection editor, noted that the organization faces challenges in establishing partnerships and that the process takes a lot of time. Our model of brand Affinity suggests that as they work to develop a clearer brand identity and develop brand Integrity, the organization will have an easier time identifying and forming the right partnerships. Identifying the right partners requires a deep self-knowledge in terms of brand identity, goals, values, and theory of change. It also requires a keen understanding of the current and potential players in an ecosystem as well as the forces and trends shaping the broader environment, as we discussed in Chapter Three.

The next step in identifying and attracting partners is to actively use the brand to attract those partners that seem most appropriate, given the organization's values, identity, and unique contribution to the theory of change. Clarity in identity and strong brand integrity helps an organization not only in identifying which partners to work with but also in attracting the right partners. Mike Boyer of Humanity United stated that "the more we can define who we are, the higher the quality of the partnership opportunities that come to us." Li Ding of NPI compared the brand "to the flag that the tour guide carries. It brings people together and attracts them so they want to be part of you and your mission." Kate Roberts of PSI noted that "we have to have a strong brand to be able to attract the right types of partners so that we can have greater impact." She also believes that to do this successfully, "you need to hang on to your own brand integrity and values." Sarah Holewinski explained that her organization strives to "build capacity partnering with people with unique skills." She concluded that "brand will help with attracting these partners."

Educate Girls is a growing nonprofit organization seeking to address gender inequality in India's educational system, reforming schools by working with multiple partners, including local communities, to increase and improve enrollment, attendance, and learning outcomes for girls. Safeena Husain, founder and CEO, believes that partnerships are the key to their success. "We have a comprehensive partnership model, and we are not territorial," she explained. "We draw from our commonalities." The organization chooses partners carefully, giving consideration to alignment of values and brand, in order to work together for financial support, curricular content, organizational development and capacity building, and monitoring and evaluation. The organization also shares credit broadly, using partners' logos for shared materials, providing website links, and acknowledging government efforts. Husain explained that given the diversity of their partners, "It is even more important to communicate what we're all about in the simplest and most direct manner." By deploying its brand with integrity, Educate Girls has built trust and gained the support of both local communities and many respected partners, such as UNICEF.

In all of these examples, high brand Integrity imparts a powerful brand image that results in trust and acts as a magnet for potential partners, and brand Affinity then leverages these partnerships to increase impact. The ability of Save the Redwoods League to stay true to its mission and values helped build the trust of other organizations, ultimately leading to more partnerships and projects, according to Jennifer Benito-Kowalski. "The fact that we are positive means people like to work with us. We are known as an environmental group that works with people to get things done. We are noticing over the last several years that people really want to partner with us. They are asking us to join bigger projects, and we are having a bigger impact."

Brand Affinity may also increasingly play a role in attracting organizations that would benefit from consolidation. We believe that there may be an increase in mergers and acquisitions in the nonprofit sector in the future, and that brand Affinity can facilitate this process. We discuss this further in Chapter Nine.

Using Brand to Manage and Add Value to Partnerships and Drive Impact

Sharing credit and promoting a partner's brand rather than one's own are examples of using brand in a collaborative way that adds value to the partnerships, promotes trust, and enhances overall impact. Jim Bildner of the Harvard Kennedy School noted that both the donor and the implementer gain from sharing credit for project successes. "For example, large foundations have very powerful brands. When these foundations commit resources and their names to an issue or project, not only are they seen as leveraging their brands to help drive the project, but all of their partner implementers also get credit for the work, and benefit from the association to the foundation's brand. There's simply no diminution of credit in these cases; everyone benefits because it is not a zero-sum game."

Not only is the promotion of partner brands the right thing to do, but as Dr. Wibulpolprasert suggests, in the long run it helps an organization "attract more partners who want to work with you and create joint impact towards social change." Thus the way an organization manages its brand partnerships can positively influence its brand image and attract further partnerships, in a kind of brand Affinity virtuous circle.

Innocent Chukwuma, executive director of the CLEEN Foundation, described a situation in which it was beneficial to give all the credit away to enhance local ownership in a community policing strategy in Nigeria. This boosted CLEEN Foundation's reputation in the country, and they found that "when we let them take credit [for] the product, they even become more generous [in terms of political action]." Mahnaz Afkhami of the Women's Learning Partnership also affirmed the importance of stepping back at times and allowing a partner's brand to stand on its own, particularly when there is a tense political climate and anti-foreign sentiments: "We are in the supporting role for our partners," she explained, "and we are perfectly understanding of when they have to make themselves sort of stand apart and boost their indigenous credentials. So there is a lot of mutual understanding of how that is done."

Partnerships were also seen as an important way of increasing brand equity, with one organization gaining credibility and building its brand through a visible relationship with a more powerful or well-respected brand. Both Tom Scott from the Gates Foundation and Yasmina Zaidman from Acumen Fund described the affirmative impact that cobranding can have for their respective partners. The Gates brand can, for example, create a positive halo effect for their grantees, helping open doors and move conversations forward. Zaidman described this effect in terms of "brand value" and noted that creative partnerships can be formed based on the value others see in joining forces with Acumen on issues of global poverty. At Humanity United, Mike Boyer experienced the same phenomenon as a beneficiary of that halo effect: "Because we are a young foundation, the more we can associate ourselves with established reputable brands, the better," he concluded.

Maximizing social impact has to do with using the brand strategically. As Robin Hogen, vice president of communications at the Robert Wood Johnson Foundation, explained, "Some foundations have more influence than money. Some punch above their weight and do a lot more with a lot less."

The examples our interviewees described depended to a large extent on the partners' being focused on a shared external social goal and feeling confident that the use of their own brand and brand assets to promote and strengthen their partner brands would indeed result in increasing the desired social impact. The challenges in managing partnerships cited by our interviewees revolved around situations in which power asymmetries existed between partners, particularly between large foundations and their grantees. Ramesh Singh, formerly of ActionAid and Open Society Foundations, for example, spoke of tensions between bigger and smaller brands, noting that bigger organizations can sometimes push their brand visibility to the detriment of their partner's brands, thereby creating resentment and dysfunction. We believe that a brand Affinity mindset can help diffuse these concerns when both partners focus on shared external goals and common social impact objectives, and when the partner with the more powerful brand makes a conscious effort to share visibility and promote its partner brands. In Chapter Nine, we will explore the role that brand Affinity plays in the growing number of movement brands, but in this chapter, we would like to share some insights about the types of brand partnerships we encountered and what makes them successful.

TYPES OF BRAND AFFINITY PARTNERSHIPS

Some of our interviewees suggested that there may be two fundamental types of partnerships of relevance for brand Affinity: those in which partner organizations are focused on similar activities (but not always identical constituents), and those in which partner organizations have the same overall goals but different activities, so that they sit either upstream or downstream of one another in the theory of change. In both cases, partners come together to increase impact, and the overall net impact of the partnership is greater than the sum of the individual organizational impacts.

For the first type of partnership, the emphasis is on joining forces to expand the resources available and to drive interest and support for a common issue or cause. This is the idea that if these nonprofits work together, all boats will float on a rising tide. Lincoln Center for the Performing Arts is a good example of an organization using its brand Affinity to help grow the number of patrons for multiple arts organizations throughout the city. This effort stemmed from detailed research focused on the attitudes and behaviors of patrons of the arts. Peter Duffin explained the findings:

> Research has shown that if someone attends more than four performances a year, they're considered an arts "heavy user" and much more likely to attend a whole range of arts events. There is a kind of tipping point for arts patrons, so it makes sense for us to collaborate with other arts organizations and share information, which is something they do in Philadelphia, and we're working on here in NYC. We think about it as growing the pie and everyone wins. It just doesn't make sense to think about art patrons in a possessive sense; they are not just Lincoln Center's customers because we share them with a wider variety of other arts organizations.

By developing a website that serves as a common portal to member organizations including the Metropolitan Opera and the New York Philharmonic, Lincoln Center has enhanced the ability of these organizations to work together. The way customers or arts patrons navigate the site, for example, demonstrates that access and exposure to one organization comes from familiarity with another member organization, and this helps Lincoln Center gain support for collaboration and joint initiatives between the member organizations.

Over the past several years, we have seen an increase in all kinds of collaborations and coalitions through which organizations with similar missions, values, theories of change, and capabilities are working together to enhance their collective brand visibility and impact. Wilmot Allen suggests that "increasingly, we are seeing a coalescence of organizations coming together and leveraging the values that their brands represent." He cited the examples of the Global Impact Investing Network and community development institutions and believes that these collaborations can also strengthen the values and identity of the organizations involved. He concluded that the "aggregation lends a certain amount of credibility and makes it easy to really see and communicate values to constituents." In this type of partnership, then, impact is increased through enhanced collective brand visibility and voice. Concurrently, those participating organizations may also gain clarity from belonging to the partnership in terms of their own brand identity. Cynthia Round, executive vice president for brand strategy and marketing at United Way Worldwide, described the credibility that comes from collaboration: "Groups of organizations get a lot more credibility because the collaborative nature attracts greater confidence in the work being done."

In the second type of partnership, complementary skills and assets can be combined to achieve an impact that neither partner acting alone could accomplish. In this case, partners leverage each other's unique skills without duplicating efforts, and the sum of the partnership is greater than the individual impact that each of the partners could have. In these partnerships, each partner plays a unique role and brings specific skills and capacities to the table to work on complex issues. Julie O'Brien commented on MSH's partnership with Oxfam: "Since Oxfam had an established name on Capitol Hill, but less implementation experience, and MSH had deep field experience but limited visibility, it was a fruitful partnership where each gained, creating greater value and leverage for their shared position, while also enhancing organizational reputation." The impact on the brand equity for each of the partners is clear.

Jeb Gutelius has found it important to "be clear about what we had and needed and what the potential partner had and needed, to find that overlap." Here again, the role of brand Integrity in defining, attracting, and managing partnerships is critical. Angelwish, an organization that supports children with chronic illness, initially saw itself as potentially competing with the Make-A-Wish Foundation. "It took a little while, but we realized we're actually very complementary, even if there is some overlap in terms of donor base," said Shimmy Mehta. The two organizations have collaborated in cases where one organization is better equipped to help a particular child than the other. "If both sides work with integrity, I think we'll see more and more of that," Mehta observed. In these types of partnerships, organizations come together to complement one another's capacities and capabilities, with the result that their combined impact is greater than the sum of the individual organization's efforts.

In both types of partnerships, brand Affinity means moving from a quid pro quo mindset to one of collective impact, and from an assumption about scarcity of resources to a belief in capacity building. In other words, brand Affinity is less about entering into a partnership for some form of transactional exchange in order to build internal organizational capacity, and more about working in a relationship with a partner, or a number of partners, to enhance collective impact. Brand Affinity is also predicated on the belief that partnerships can increase capacity and access to resources. The Girl Effect is a striking example of brand Affinity: organizational partners were actively involved from the beginning in developing and implementing the brand, each partner playing the role to which it was best suited. Early on, the participation of BRAC, CARE, and the Population Council helped shape the organization's theory of change; these partners also provided data, stories, and support for messaging. What has been particularly interesting is the recognition by these organizations that the partnership also has been a vehicle for them to influence each other in a positive manner, helping each become a more effective organization. If these organizations had operated under a model that assumed they were all competitors, the same impact would not have been possible (Kylander, 2011).

Although some of our interviewees considered partnerships with corporations to be potentially risky, others believed them to be an important way to influence change. Stephanie Kurzina described Oxfam's complex relationship with corporate partners, expanding on both the benefits and risks of these. "With global corporations that have all sorts of subsidiaries, you might be campaigning against a subsidiary, and that endangers your relationship with the corporate parent, so it's very tricky," she explained. "We want to be open minded about these partnerships because we recognize that corporations are huge players in the whole set of issues on which we work every day. They are the potential creators or alleviators of poverty, they can contribute to eradicating injustice, and we want to influence them, through our partnerships, to take positive action." In examples like these that are cross sector in nature but still based on complementary skills, the role of the brand can extend to actually influencing partners' behavior and activities so as to increase positive social and often economic impact. We believe that companies will continue to be interested in addressing social and environmental issues and that this affords nonprofit organizations a tremendous opportunity to influence the behavior and activities of companies through partnerships and brand Affinity.

SOURCES OF SUCCESS FOR BRAND AFFINITY

Organizations (and individuals) with congruent or similar theories of change are more likely to be able to find common ground and collaborate successfully together. Theories of change are often based on explicit and implicit values and beliefs that, when shared with other organizations, serve as a basis for trust and collaboration. As John Hammock, associate professor of public policy at the Fletcher School at Tufts University, noted, "You have to pick your partners wisely." He added that "one of the real problems with partnerships is not spending enough time before the partnership takes place, to actually make sure you're all in agreement and share the same values and goals." Partners that do not share values and goals can present a risk. As David Wood, director of the initiative for responsible investment at the Hauser Institute for Civil

Society at Harvard University, cautioned, if organizations engage in partnerships that are not a good fit in terms of shared values, they may be "forced into decisions around ownership of ideas and projects that may lead to mission drift, decreased capacity, and potentially a compromised brand." How well partner brands fit is therefore to some extent an indication of brand Affinity success. Kees de Graaf of Twaweza believes that "the brand, 'Twaweza: Ni Sisi!' or 'We can do it: it's us!' is very important [in] choosing partners. When we partner, we help people understand what we are about and what we believe in and look for overlapping views, a win-win situation." In conclusion, as Tom Scott argued, "The good brand Affinity relationships are the ones that have very clear goals that each side is trying to achieve, and there's a kind of mutual agreement that there is a set of end outcomes that matter. Unsuccessful relationships are where there is not a clear tieback to the work, mission, or outcome we're trying to achieve." Sharing similar values and goals and actively working to create trust are two important bases for successful partnerships.

A good example of the role of values in driving brand Affinity is that of Educate Girls. The organization's core value is respect—respect for all partners, including the government. When concerns are raised about services that the government should be providing, the organization encourages the government to follow existing legal requirements, without being antagonistic. This respectful approach builds trust, enabling the organization to create effective partnerships with government, local community members, and other organizations. This in turn supports the organization's strategy, which relies on village-level implementation and local volunteers, and builds a brand image that further attracts partnerships. As Nooreen Dossa, communications manager for Educate Girls, explained, "The most important role of our brand is to invite all stakeholders to feel like a part of the organization and its goals."

In the case of networks and coalitions, the process of defining shared values and goals can be important in and of itself. Mahnaz Afkhami of the Women's Learning Partnership described the process of creating a shared vision and identity internally so as to guide a network of autonomous NGOs in external engagements with their constituencies and in broader efforts to effect social change. "One aspect of [branding] is for us as a group of independent autonomous organizations to come to [a] shared vision that we truly internalize . . . It took us a number of years to have that; and it involves considerable conversation to come to trust each other, to deeply believe in each other's capabilities, and [have] respect for that." In this case, the process of building a collective brand identity was fundamental to the success of the network itself.

Using the brand in a collaborative way to add value to partners and sharing visibility and credit generously also promote an atmosphere of trust, which is fundamental for successful partnerships. For CARE, under the leadership of Peter Bell, this meant "not being the leader, but being a partner of choice . . . which also means a willingness to listen to others and to work with them toward shared goals; to build an open, candid, and mutually trustful relationship; and to share the credit for advances and the responsibility for setbacks." For Dr. Wibulpolprasert, "fostering a spirit of trust, where partners and their contributions are valued and shared in the larger quest towards social change," is an essential factor of successful brand partnerships. Chris Helfrich of Nothing But Nets noted the importance of trust in building partnerships with organizations that occupy the same space. Part of the success of these partnerships is that organizations generally take on complementary roles. This works, he said, when the organization "occupies a very specific niche and has a partnership mentality." "The challenge," noted Kathy Viatella, managing director of programs at Sustainable Conservation, "is to define roles and take credit for the work, especially when funders are involved. It requires tremendous partnership-building efforts to establish trust." Sharing credit and developing trust are therefore fundamental to building successful relationships and partnerships. In Chapter Five we articulated how brand Integrity also helps establish and promote this trust.

Finally, the use of data to prove the value of brand Affinity and support collaboration, in terms of both impact and increased effectiveness and efficiency, was seen as an important source of success. Lincoln Center, in the collaborative effort described earlier, included a number of organizations both big and small, and initially, some organizations were more skeptical of the value of working together. "We really had to prove the value of collaboration," explained Peter Duffin, describing how the research data helped them achieve that and implement brand Affinity successfully.

AN OPEN-SOURCE AND FLEXIBLE APPROACH TO THE USE OF BRAND ASSETS

Making brand assets and tools available to partners, either through targeted sharing or more widely through open-source platforms, facilitates collaboration, expanding the reach and impact of brands using a brand Affinity approach. For Alexis Ettinger of the Skoll Centre for Social Entrepreneurship at Oxford University, brand openness and flexibility is a way to invite collaboration and honor different stakeholder perspectives, conceptualizing what they do as a part of a "collaborative hub." For Elizabeth Benedict of Social Venture Partners (SVP), being open and sharing brand assets are key strategies for driving impact. "We even have some strategic partners in the SVP network that are using our messaging and brand materials," she explained. "The more porous we are, the more reach we have. For example, one of our beneficiaries, a staff member of one of our nonprofit investees, was talking about his work with SVP publically, and he used the same brand language we use, so it's permeating everywhere. We feel that the more open we are with the brand, the more adoption we will get yet still be true to the brand framework."

Mayur Paul, communications and brand manager at HelpAge International, concurs, adding that "freeing the brand" can actually help win people to a cause and increase momentum. "Have a good idea and make sure the organization lives the idea. When people steal it, it's a good thing," he asserted. "Letting others run with your brand will make it more powerful and increase your reach." Will Novy-Hildesley noted how interesting the branding process becomes once you give up control over the brand and allow partners to access brand assets. He believes that this process "can have impact beyond your direct work using your brand." Pam Brandin, executive director of the Vista Center for the Blind and Visually Impaired, explained the process of letting go: "I went from being a careful brand policewoman to letting just about any of our constituents use our logo, mission, tagline, pillars, etc. Everyone wants to do their best to be consistent—they all helped create our image, and now they want to maintain it." Although there was reluctance to release the brand, there is now greater commitment from other stakeholders to support it. We believe that this approach to sharing brand assets with partners increases transparency, deepens the relationships, and promotes trust.

Jack Sim described how the World Toilet Organization works through multiple partnerships to improve sanitation conditions for people globally. The brand is focused on raising awareness of this issue and reducing inhibitions in talking about the subject. The nonprofit does this in provocative ways, referring to bodily waste using a popular slang term and injecting both humor and seriousness into discussions. "Our goal is to have everyone join in and talk about it," explained Sim. "We want to let everyone own the brand in their own way. If you are open in this way, then everyone comes, superstars and average people. You can mobilize millions of people by getting them to own the brand and issue," he added. "You have to be able to widely disseminate and tweet this thing. A social movement can mobilize a wide variety of people and reflects a belief in the system that truly goes beyond the organization."

In many ways, this open and flexible approach to brand management is similar to brand Democracy, and results in some of the same benefits of increased engagement and buy-in. Meghan Reddick of YMCA Canada noted that once the organization had developed brand tools to share internally using technology platforms, extending these same tools beyond traditional organizational boundaries to volunteers, suppliers, vendors, and other organizations just makes sense. "We don't want to put the products of our brand work under lock and key," she stated. "We want to extend them as tools for everyone who wants to promote the YMCA brand. Staff, volunteers, partners, suppliers are all invited to sign up to our new internal brand website. Then everyone also feels a responsibility to build and protect the brand." Driven by a similar mindset of openness and collaboration, a number of nonprofit organizations are actively sharing their knowledge and aspects of their brand work in the hope that other organizations will replicate their approach and, by proxy, scale their impact. As Sasha Chanoff of RefugePoint noted, "We want to create replicable models that can open up avenues for other organizations to do similar work to ours . . . We want to continue to build collaborations. Our goal is not to increase market share, but to expand the resettlement effort and numbers overall." Kees de Graaf of Twaweza summed it up by saying that "for a company where the goal is to protect the brand [for use only by that company], it's different. We want other organizations to take our up our brand and increase its exposure."

Many of the successful movement brands we encountered, as well as a number of organizational brands such as SVP and YMCA Canada, were based on open-source platforms where the brand visuals, data, and supporting materials could be freely accessed by anyone. The open-source nature of both the Girl Effect and TckTckTck brands allowed for different organizations and individuals to take and adapt the brands according to their own local contexts and needs. Christian Teriete, who worked on TckTckTck, reflected on this approach: "Usually, I guess this [open sourcing] is a no-go in branding, but all this was tolerated because, I think, the idea was really to unite as much of civil society, all sorts of activists and movements that were out there and cared somehow about climate change, and create this impression that all of these social movements and groups were united under one banner."

In the case of the Girl Effect, an effort to promote support for the potential of adolescent girls to end poverty (created by the Nike Foundation, in collaboration with NoVo Foundation, United Nations Foundation, and Coalition for Adolescent Girls), evolved into a movement that recognizes girls as "the most powerful force for change on the planet." The Girl Effect brand has garnered broad interest, support, and awareness from organizations and individuals across the globe through compelling videos and materials freely accessible to all. Interest and awareness exploded after Oprah Winfrey aired the Girl Effect videos on her show and a Girl Effect video won the TED Ads Worth Watching Award. It became a challenge to determine how to harness this interest. "Our first call to action for everyone was: spread the word," explained Emily Brew, former creative director at the Nike Foundation. By linking with other partners, including GlobalGiving, interested donors could find projects to support in the developing world. The model of open-source materials, including access to downloadable videos, logos, photographs, posters, presentations, and suggestions for how to run a Girl Effect party or event, made it easy for interested individuals to become involved and communicate the brand through their own actions. "We wanted something that people could get behind and make their own," explained Maria Eitel (Kylander, 2011, p. 6). This approach is clear on the website, which encourages people to create their own folder of Girl Effect materials or download everything at once. "This site is yours," it stipulates. "Take the information and tools you need to change the world for girls."

An open and flexible sharing of brand assets and tools may initially seem risky and even counterintuitive; but when an organization is focused on driving a particular social impact and generating support using brand Affinity, placing brand assets in service of these partners and the overall goal makes a lot of sense. The team that created the Girl Effect noted that there are some risks to an open-source brand. With the viral spread of messages, there was backlash from some audiences. Brew described how external audiences took on a role that went beyond being brand ambassadors, whereby supporters were actually helping define strategies to respond to this negative pushback. "We didn't have to come up with all the solutions. We could crowdsource them." Although Brew acknowledged that there is an inherent risk in providing open access to materials, as materials can be misappropriated, she believes that the benefits outweigh the risks.

CHALLENGES OF BRAND AFFINITY

Brand Affinity, particularly for brand managers with backgrounds in the private sector, can feel counterintuitive and risky. In essence, brand Affinity supports using an organization's brand equity and assets to promote issues and organizational entities that lie outside the organizational boundaries and control. As a result, it is possible that a short-term decrease in organizational visibility and awareness can occur. Longer term, being part of collaborative efforts can actually increase brand visibility. Some of our interviewees expressed concern that brand Affinity would dilute their own brand's equity; some were nervous that their organizations and their brands would become lost; and others felt that a brand Affinity approach would represent an unjustified drain on time and resources. We address these three concerns in this section.

Diluting Brand Equity

In traditional private sector brand equity models, brand equity is driven by awareness and customer loyalty. The concern is that brand Affinity could potentially reduce awareness, particularly on the part of the general public. But as we discussed in Chapter Two, for nonprofits, brand equity is driven by trust, partnerships, consistency, and focus. Trust stems from brand Integrity, and partnerships, as we have argued, are supported by a brand Affinity approach. Consistency and focus may be challenging to achieve over time and across geographies, but they are in no way compromised—indeed, we believe that they are strengthened—by brand Affinity. Once again, concerns around dilution of brand equity are anchored in the old brand paradigm and the differences between the nonprofit and private sectors. We believe that brand equity for nonprofit organizations is enhanced by the implementation of the brand IDEA and that partnerships, one of the key drivers of brand equity in nonprofits, are strongly supported by a brand Affinity approach.

Losing Yourself and Your Brand in Affinity

Some organizations worry that if they dive too deeply into brand Affinity and partnerships and collaborations, they will either lose a sense of themselves or be "hijacked" by another organization. These are legitimate concerns that highlight why it is critical at the outset for organizations to be firmly rooted in their own sense of brand identity and to choose their partners proactively and with a view to enhancing their impact and mission implementation. We have come across situations where a smaller organization's brand is defined only in connection with its much larger partner's brand. Although this may have some benefits in terms of lending legitimacy to the smaller organization, it can also undermine the ability of that smaller partner to build its own distinctive brand. You must therefore be clear about who you are and clearly define your goals for the partnerships you choose to engage in. Brand affinity helps you achieve exactly this. By positioning for clarity and proactively seeking partners that help further your mission and desired impact, you can actually use brand Affinity to enhance and strengthen your own brand identity.

Preventing the Drain on Time and Resources

It is true that managing a successful portfolio of partners takes time and resources, and organizations may worry that this can interfere with focusing on their own organizational needs. But as we have argued, partnerships can also be thought of in terms of assets that add to the capacity of an organization and enable it to better implement its mission and increase its impact. All assets, including partnerships, must be acquired, managed, and maintained. Brand Affinity can support organizations in selecting, managing, and leveraging their partnership assets and can be thought of as an investment in capacity building rather than as a drain on resources.

SUMMARY

Organizations that adopt a brand Affinity approach believe that this is the most effective and efficient way to maximize impact and implement their mission. As we have seen, brand Affinity requires strong brand Integrity and a focus on shared external goals. Organizations demonstrating brand Affinity use their brand to identify and attract partners and to add value to these partners and the collaborative endeavor. It takes time to build trust, but by sharing credit generously and focusing on the joint external goals, organizations can leverage their brands to promote partnerships and drive social change. A brand Affinity approach is in some ways an extension of brand Democracy and entails sharing brand tools and assets with partners with the objective of maximizing overall impact.

Having read about the three components of the brand IDEA framework in some detail in this chapter and Chapters Five and Six, you can clearly see that brand Integrity, brand Democracy, and brand Affinity are interrelated and mutually supportive. It is difficult to achieve brand Integrity without the participative process of brand Democracy. At the same time, it is only by working on brand Integrity that you can effectively empower brand ambassadors and create guiding principles for brand management, which represent additional aspects of brand Democracy. Brand Affinity is what you do with your brand to maximize your organization's impact, after you have achieved brand Integrity through brand Democracy. In the next chapter, we provide some guidelines and suggestions for the implementation of the brand IDEA as a whole.

PART

3

PUTTING THE
BRAND IDEA
INTO ACTION

CHAPTER

8

IMPLEMENTING THE BRAND IDEA

What to Do and How to Do It

Now that we have introduced the three concepts of the brand IDEA, we move to a discussion of how to put this framework into action. We have gained a deeper understanding of the role of brand and the brand IDEA framework through our research and interviews with the organizations whose voices permeate the preceding chapters, and this chapter builds on that learning and experience. These organizations have taken a variety of approaches to strengthening their brand and using their brand in strategic ways to further their mission and drive social impact. A number of organizations we interviewed have already incorporated the brand IDEA concepts into their rebranding efforts, using the article in the *Stanford Social Innovation Review* or one of a number of webinars and presentations that we held over the course of 2012. Others have been at the forefront of brand Democracy and brand Affinity, and their work has shaped the concepts in the brand IDEA. Still others have struggled with managing their brand and have reflected long and hard on how brand can increase impact for their organizations. We drew on all these examples to develop a series of concrete recommendations and guidelines based on what we perceive to be some current best practices in the implementation of the brand IDEA framework.

We divide our recommendations into two overarching themes: (1) implementing brand Integrity through brand Democracy, and (2)

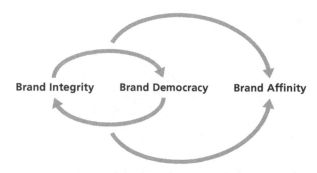

FIGURE 8.1. *Interrelationship of Brand Integrity, Brand Democracy, and Brand Affinity*

creating brand Affinity for impact. As we have noted, these concepts are all interrelated (see Figure 8.1). We also offer some measurement tools, based on the Role of Brand Cycle, that organizations can use to assess the impact of their brand management efforts.

The first step in implementing the brand IDEA is to fully embrace the paradigm shift. If leadership shifts its thinking about brand to a strategic mindset focused on mission, participative engagement, and collaboration, then brand management becomes part of daily activities. Brand management does not require large budgets or expensive external consultants. Indeed, the fundamentally dynamic nature of organizations demands that to stay relevant, they must continuously evolve as their macro and micro environments change and as new ideas, strategies, and programs are designed and implemented in response to audience needs. Staying tuned in to your audiences and keeping abreast of what different players in your micro environment are doing and how you are perceived relative to them are continuous organizational imperatives for effective brand management. Building this capacity internally as part of everyone's agenda, rather than relying on external consultants, will ensure that your organization and its brand stay relevant. We believe that this is something that all organizations can do. External consultants can certainly be helpful, but much of what we recommend can be done by the organization itself, either as part of daily activities or by specific designated teams. Smaller, more resource-constrained organizations are increasingly able to talk to their constituents in a variety of ways, and all organizations stand to benefit from an open-source approach to brand management.

We recognize that some organizations may find it useful to hire consultants to support their work on brand. Consultants can add value in a variety of ways, from helping to conduct the necessary research to structuring and facilitating a rebranding process. We want to stress, however, that one of the keys to a strong brand is incorporating the principle of brand Democracy, and organizations that hire consultants without also engaging in this type of participatory process may find that they do not get the results they desire. A brand developed without broad participation will not be as strong, nor will it be adopted as successfully, as one that is built through the principle of brand Democracy.

IMPLEMENT BRAND INTEGRITY THROUGH BRAND DEMOCRACY

The brand IDEA can be useful for framing the discussion and process of brand management. For example, during their recent strategic planning effort, the leadership of the Public Education Foundation recognized the need to rebrand the organization. Christa Payne, vice president of external affairs, and Shannon Edmondson, development and communications officer, related how the organization was in the middle of this process when they came across our SSIR article on the role of brand. Payne explained,

> What the brand IDEA did was to help us frame brand in a completely different way. We ran a meeting using the IDEA framework and emphasizing the need for brand Democracy and the importance of mission. This was really helpful because before, when we had started to discuss internally how to restructure and rebrand, barriers went up. But when we started by talking about the mission and getting a dialogue going on how to actualize that, everyone felt a lot more comfortable. We emphasized that [brand identity] is about using our mission to center and talk about our work.

And Edmondson continued,

> The IDEA framework was a great on-ramp. We had been working on this for eight months and getting to a point where people were ready to give up. But the acronym and words like "democracy" and "affinity" helped us reframe the whole discussion. I don't want to suggest it was easy, but it was a way of moving from a prescriptive process to something that engaged people and got their participation and comfort levels way up.

Our hope is that the brand IDEA framework can serve as an "on-ramp" to guide many other organizations in managing their brand. Our recommendations for implementing brand Integrity through brand

Democracy encompass three sets of activities: conducting research and assessments, driving alignment, and engaging brand ambassadors. Although we discuss them separately, these activities are interrelated; they are not once-and-done, sequential steps.

Conduct Research and Assessments

Conducting research to understand how your organization and its brand are perceived, as well as who the main audiences and ecosystem players are, is fundamental to good brand management. You are certainly already conducting research on an ongoing basis by listening and exchanging information with colleagues and staying up-to-date on the trends, forces, and changing actors influencing your sector. Here we offer some ideas and suggestions for formalizing this research as it specifically pertains to your brand. The resulting data can both provide the impetus to implement the brand IDEA and shape your brand management efforts.

Know Who You Are and How You Are Perceived

Knowing who you are as an organization, what you do, and why it matters is the key to being able to articulate brand identity. Understanding how you are perceived, particularly by external stakeholders, is important to defining your existing brand image. This means asking internal and external stakeholders what they believe to be the essence of your brand. This type of research can be described as a brand audit. An internal brand audit comprises both the research on how internal stakeholders think and talk about the brand identity and a review of all the ways in which the brand is expressed and communicated in both visual and verbal terms. An external brand audit comprises research on how external stakeholders perceive the brand image as well as how the organization is portrayed by the media and other external sources, such as rating organizations.

As a first step in conducting a brand audit, use brainstorming sessions to ask internal stakeholders (board members, managers, staff, and volunteers) to articulate "who we are, what we do, and why it's important." At a recent faculty meeting at the Hauser Institute for Civil Society at Harvard University, we went around the table asking individuals to define in their own words, and in less than sixty seconds, what they believed the Hauser Institute's identity to be. Although there were some differences, there were more similarities and some clear overarching themes.

Another approach is to ask stakeholders to take a few minutes to jot down on a piece of paper the six or seven key words that best describe their organization. When we ask nonprofit leaders to do this and then ask them whether their colleagues or other internal stakeholders would use similar descriptors, we often observe some hesitation. Executives tell us, "That's the first thing I am going to do—ask my team how they would define our brand."

You must also engage external stakeholders (donors, partners, beneficiaries, and supporters) by asking them through interviews, focus groups, or informal discussions how they would describe the organization and what they feel are the organization's key strengths and weaknesses. Through capturing and defining perceived brand image, you can understand to what extent the brand identity and image are aligned and gain insight into aspects of brand identity and support for branding processes. Kate Roberts of PSI described an issue faced by many nonprofits: "When an organization has good donors, is doing well, and is having an impact, there is little impetus to build the organization's brand. The assumption is that the results will speak for themselves." The reality, however, is that all organizations need to be actively managing their brand, as PSI recognized when it conducted a brand audit and found a mismatch between internal and external perceptions. This information, along with the common themes that emerged from research on perceptions, helped form the basis for brand identity.

The United Way uses online focus groups, public opinion polls, and other qualitative data to understand external perceptions and opinions of its brand. In this way, it anchors its discussions and decisions in consumer-based information. This "gets you out of the subjective into the objective," explains Cynthia Round, "which helps attract resources and support to do branding work."

You must also mine existing program data to help clarify brand identity so that it reflects not only the mission but also the realities in the field. Barakat used data from the field to anchor its rebranding process. This included statistics on where programs were located and who was being served, and an evaluation of the local impact. "The data coming from our programs in the field all pointed to the fact that our schools were only in Pakistan and Afghanistan and that we were reaching children and women, especially girls—so we needed to come out and say that!" explained Angha Childress. She added that "brand has to be driven from the inside." At Special Olympics, the organization started its brand realignment with a discovery phase. Kirsten Suto Seckler explained, "We needed to discover every facet of how the brand was being implemented, used, and visualized, across the organization both historically and where we were today." This research helped shape the foundation for the rebranding initiative.

Understand Key Audiences and How You Fit in the Ecosystem

Identifying and understanding the needs of key audiences is another important area for research and assessment. This concept overlaps with that of knowing who you are and how you are perceived. But the difference here is that the research is focused on understanding, across audiences, your differentiation and positioning relative to other players. It is important to segment your external audiences and reach out to them through meetings, focus groups, surveys, and informal discussions so as to clearly understand their needs and their perceptions of your brand relative to other players in the ecosystem. Tom Scott provided an example of how this was done at the Gates Foundation: "We put in place an audience taxonomy as a jumping-off point, broad categories, then segmented by geography, demographics, and psychographics. None of this can be successful," he added, "if you are not crystal clear about who your audiences are, what you want them to do, and what the desired outcomes are. If you don't know your audience, you can't tailor how you want to work or communicate with them."

Understanding the other players in the space and mapping the relative strengths of different organizations help clarify how your organization fits within its ecosystem. Data on the strength of your brand relative to other players can also help you gain support and traction for brand initiatives throughout your own organization. YMCA Canada, a federation with a national office and fifty-one member associations that are independent charities, conducted some research on YMCA's brand strength relative to other Canadian nonprofits. "This had the benefit of showing everyone that our brand was not as strong as it should have been and that brand is an important asset worthy of protection," explained Meghan Reddick. "We built a case using the data for why we should invest in the brand."

Articulating the organization's theory of change is essential not only for clarifying brand identity but also for understanding how an organization relates to potential partners for brand Affinity. A theory of change should describe the process by which the desired social impact will be achieved, including the means by which inputs and activities such as resources, programs, and services will effect change, and any assumptions about causality. The theory of change here is not so much used as a tool for performance evaluation, as is often the case, but more as a diagnostic tool for understanding the unique contributions of individual organizations as a precursor to identifying potential partners.

In short, conducting research and assessment needs to be part of an ongoing process to manage the brand. Engaging and understanding both internal and external audiences allows managers to better define brand identity, understand brand image, and gain clarity as to what extent these are aligned. Table 8.1 summarizes key suggested activities for conducting brand research and assessments. Data from research also helps create support and direction for branding initiatives. As Scott said, "Today we know much more about our brand, much more about all of our audiences, and we know perceptions on major attributes and issues." To paraphrase Sir Francis Bacon's assertion that knowledge is power, research is what enables organizations to build powerful brands.

Drive Alignment

We define brand Integrity as the alignment between the brand identity and the organization's mission, values, and strategy and between brand identity and brand image. A clear and accurate mission is a vital element in achieving alignment. We believe that every nonprofit should strive to maintain up-to-date mission, vision, and values statements that are widely disseminated both internally and externally. We have observed that when you do not have an effective mission statement that accurately reflects your organization's work, you are unable to achieve a clear brand identity. Jeb Gutelius suggested that nonprofits should be "taking the time at the beginning [of a branding effort] to work through values, mission, and vision. These things are really easy to read, but not easy to create." He added, "It has been important for me to slow down and define the guiding principles that should come through in all of the work that we do. By trying to cement those pillars early on, you can better guide the organization."

Connect Brand to Organizational Mission, Values, and Strategy

The organizations that best demonstrate the concepts of the brand IDEA view their brand as directly connected to their mission, values, and strategy. The brand is anchored in the "who, what, and why" of the organization. The mission statement and values are often the starting point for framing the brand identity, but connecting the brand to the mission can be hard work that requires a participative process and willingness to engage in potentially challenging discussions.

Many organizations drive alignment by directly linking their rebranding effort with their strategic planning efforts. Childfund is an example of an organization that identified the core intent of the brand based on its new strategy. As Anne Goddard described, "In the past, when the brand needed a facelift, consultants would try to uncover the essence of the organization, but they never got it. When we did it (the

TABLE 8.1. *Conduct Research and Assessments*

What to Do	How to Do It	Tools and Tactics
Know who you are and how you are perceived	• Ask internal stakeholders how they talk about your organization and define brand identity • Ask external stakeholders how they view your organization • Collect data from operations and programs	• Schedule brainstorming sessions, invite input through surveys and interviews, ask internal stakeholders what words they use to describe your organization • Use focus groups, surveys, and informal interviews to ask external stakeholders about the strengths and weaknesses of your organization and how they perceive your brand • Gather activity, output, and outcome data • Conduct a brand audit, analyzing perceptions, reviewing materials that express and communicate the brand, and tracking what external organizations are saying (rating organizations, press coverage)
Understand key audiences and how you fit in the ecosystem	• Segment your audiences to understand their needs and perceptions • Map out a clear theory of change	• Define and group audiences based on shared interests and characteristics • Conduct focus groups, surveys, interviews, and informal discussions to assess their needs and perceptions of your organization relative to other players • Define and articulate the causal relationships and assumptions by which social impact is achieved in the theory of change, and the specific role your organization plays within this theory of change

brand and strategy together), staff said, "I get it now!" Goddard was surprised that their results have been so positive and the brand has been so widely accepted. She attributes the success to the fact that people participated in the organizational strategy and were part of its development, and embracing the brand followed directly from this integrated, participatory effort.

We believe you can incorporate branding into your strategic planning efforts using a participative process. Many organizations with whom we spoke created a steering committee for their work on brand. In small organizations, the management team may play this role. The key is to incorporate appropriate representation from across the organization in order to engage broad participation.

For Publish What You Pay (PWYP), the integration of brand into the strategic planning process is captured in a living document titled Vision 20/20, which describes the organization's strategy for 2012–2016, its mission, theory of change, operating principles and standards, brand guidelines, and governance structure. Vision 20/20 is based on four strategic pillars, one of which, called "Practice What We Preach," directly reflects the concept of aligning the brand with values. "PWYP's brand and logo must continue to be associated with integrity, quality, and excellence," explained Marinke van Riet.

There is often a tendency to postpone work on the brand until the organization revisits its mission or strategy. This, we think, is a mistake. Work on these issues needs to go hand in hand or be linked directly with rebranding efforts. Brand should not be an afterthought. When the Melton Foundation developed a new mission for the organization as part of its strategy work, the leadership and staff believed that external audiences would understand it easily. According to Winthrop Carty, executive director, this wasn't the case. The confusion led management to further assess how the brand was perceived and experienced by stakeholders. Management then worked to align the brand with the new mission. In retrospect, Carty recognized that these elements—strategy, mission, and brand—might have been addressed more efficiently together at the outset. Although some organizations do these processes sequentially, we believe they should be closely linked and integrated.

We want to emphasize that brand identity not only reflects the organization as it is today but also incorporates what the organization aspires to become, which can be based on both the mission itself and the organizational vision. Your internal discussions and brainstorming around brand identity should include room for an aspirational identity based on organizational vision.

Align Brand Identity and Image

Aligning identity and image is not a single discrete step; it represents an ongoing process that occurs as an organization works on identity and learns and integrates information regarding its image. We believe that both the participative process and the external data and perspectives mentioned earlier are critical to reaching consensus on brand identity and aligning it with brand image. Sybil Wailand, managing partner at Consumer Dynamics, shared examples in her work as a consultant where internal discussions on brand were unable to really move forward until input about external perceptions was injected. "With multiple audiences, it is important to hear everyone's voice. Giving internal audiences a chance to convey their points of view and to listen to each other really opens the door to greater understanding. Furthermore, when we expose each point of view to external stakeholders through focus groups and interviews, the objective learning internal audiences get from that experience helps move them away from individual biases and clearly see what is most compelling for the brand." The iterative process of exposing and testing each hypothesis helps an organization reach consensus.

Alignment is achieved through this broad participation of both external and internal stakeholders. Wilmot Allen has found in his work with a number of nonprofits that incorporating the perspective of external constituents through a structured mechanism builds understanding and supports alignment. He shared an example in which a public charter school established a parents' union to give constituents a voice and ownership over the brand. The school also hired parents on their staff to better understand their needs as stakeholders in their children's education. Allen sees such inclusion as key to programmatic success, and "[although] not every nonprofit will be able to hire people representing their constituency, the same can be achieved through an advisory board or other ad hoc tools in a way that has substance and integrates them into the program." It is important to "find ways in which the interests of external constituencies can be incorporated into internal discussions of brand identity."

Once alignment is achieved, you must continue to monitor perceptions and address any misperceptions that arise. The Ford Foundation acknowledged that maintaining brand alignment takes work. "Alignment is fundamental," explained Marta Tellado, "but you have to intentionally and actively work at that. It's constant. You never reach the point where you can say, 'OK, we've achieved alignment, we're done.' It's dynamic and continuing." Building an ongoing process to gather external perspectives and provide the space and time for broad participation of stakeholders is an important element for managing your brand.

TABLE 8.2. *Drive Alignment*

What to Do	How to Do It	Tools and Tactics
Connect brand to organizational mission, values, and strategy	• Anchor all brand discussions in terms of your organization's mission and values • Explicitly integrate brand into your strategy and strategic planning processes	• Engage stakeholders in discussing the who, what, and why of your organization • Include assessment of brand in analysis for strategic planning, and incorporate the brand in your strategic documents
Align brand identity and image	• Establish a participative process for driving alignment • Use external research and data to drive internal discussions • Broadly disseminate and communicate your new or updated brand identity	• Establish a steering committee with broad representation to work on the brand • Integrate external stakeholders, such as donors and beneficiaries, in brand meetings and committees • Integrate the data from focus groups and surveys of both internal and external stakeholders, finding the common themes based on mission or values • Update visual identity

As you strive toward brand Integrity, your communications then need to emanate from this place of alignment. Public Education Foundation reoriented its brand to focus on "transforming public education," which has brought together stakeholders from elementary, middle, and high schools to collaborate on the foundation's mission to increase student achievement so that all students succeed in learning and in life. Christa Payne described what a difference the rebranding has made in their communications efforts. "In previous communications, we always used to lead with what we do. But since we all do different things and focus on different aspects of our work, it got confusing. By focusing on our values and what we believe in, we are all on the same page. We know who we are, and everyone in the organization knows how they fit in and what part they play. So we don't just talk about what we do anymore, but we always lead with what we believe in and then we go into how our activities support our mission." When you communicate this aligned brand identity and image then you continue to reinforce and strengthen your brand.

The alignment may, but does not have to, include a redesign of the visual identity. As we have said, brand is much more than a logo. However, many organizations adapt their visual identity to their new aligned understanding of their brand. At Barakat, once Angha Childress integrated the input from their participative process into a new mission statement and brand identity, the organization worked on developing the visual representation of this identity. She found two graphic design interns who helped create a visual identity, tapping into the history of the organization, which was founded by rug merchants and which operates in areas where the rug trade continues to play an important role. "The new identity is the word Barakat ('blessing') with some design elements that echo our history (rug patterns and colors). Education is the blessing; education brings about the peace that we need in the world. This is who we are to the communities in which we work." Testing the visual identity with the target audiences should be part of your ongoing process to inform and monitor your brand. Table 8.2 summarizes key suggested activities for driving alignment by connecting the brand to organizational mission, values, and strategy and aligning brand identity and image.

Support Brand Ambassadors

Brand Democracy gives rise to an authentic and powerful brand identity as well as brand Integrity and organizational cohesion. This occurs when your organization engages internal and external stakeholders and decentralizes responsibility for brand communications. Providing training and support and promoting the use of stories are all important activities to help achieve this engagement.

Engage Internal Stakeholders

Many organizations we spoke with are building a capacity for internal branding by educating internal stakeholders on the concepts of brand and brand management. Brand Democracy, however, goes beyond internal branding to actively engage internal (and external) audiences in defining and communicating the organization's brand.

In organizations that have resisted the notion of brand management until now, education needs to start with communicating what a brand is and why it is important. Using the discussion of the paradigm shift in Chapter One as part of this education may be helpful. Changing the culture of an organization and shifting the mindset to view brand as a strategic asset take time. YMCA Canada started its rebranding process with an extensive internal branding effort. "Our approach," explained Meghan Reddick, "was really to coach and teach, and to help everyone understand brand value. To do this we had to provide some training and education on what a brand is." This education has led to a cultural shift in the organization. "People here used to think that brand is what you do afterwards as a kind of an add-on to make something 'look' good. We have switched the culture and shifted people's understanding so that they now start with the brand positioning and everything flows from that."

The participative process of brand Democracy should be ongoing. By holding regular education and training for internal stakeholders, you can help them internalize your brand and convey it authentically on a daily basis through the work they do. As Mayur Paul at HelpAge International described to us, "Staff members are our brand. Most people experience our brand through our staff, not the website or ads." The organization invests time in training and educating staff on the mission and the brand. "We strive to make sure our staff believes in the mission so that fifteen members from fifteen different countries could convey the same message about what HelpAge is." This does not mean having identical speeches. Each individual needs to find his or her own words to convey the who, what, and why of the organization. The goal is to have consistency but not necessarily uniformity in reflecting the mission and values of the organization. BRAC also recognizes the importance of a continuous internal branding process, according to Asif Saleh. "We are laying out the principles of the brand and what BRAC stands for and training people in the organization on these principles." You need a clear training plan both to educate new employees and to continually reinforce concepts with existing employees.

The YMCA used multiple approaches to achieve this broad participation and engage internal audiences. "Every member was involved and invited to submit data on their brand," explained Reddick. "We used an external consultant and core teams; internal support in the form of tools, practical advice, and information about branding; as well as a series of educational webinars. We hosted a brand camp conference, inviting participants from every member association to convene for three days to learn everything to do with branding. We also struck a brand council, made up of experts from our associations, to participate in developing the strategy." Each member association designated a brand lead who became a champion of the branding efforts and identified brand team members. The CEOs of member organizations were directly targeted for training and involvement as well. "There is more sharing of resources between our member associations as a result," reflected Reddick, "and I think this branding process may serve as a template for future organization-wide initiatives."

In order to successfully manage your brand through brand Democracy, you need to take time and energy to create ongoing opportunities for education, training, and support. You can use a variety of formats, such as brown bags, retreats, educational and brainstorming sessions, and role-playing exercises. Designate specific people as brand champions and create brand teams composed of individuals from different parts of the organization, including volunteers, to stimulate more active engagement. Twaweza employs several different formats for educating staff, including in-depth learning sessions, a reading club, an annual immersion when all staff live with host families up-country for a week, "food for thought" (brown bag) lunches, and an annual retreat. Swami Vivekananda Youth Movement holds regular trainings for both new and existing employees in which they talk about the organization's work and the brand, and at Save the Redwoods League, "Brand is part of everything that we do," explained Jennifer Benito-Kowalski. "We try to do it in a fun way, holding brand quizzes during staff meetings."

Many of the tools we have just described encourage internal stakeholders to communicate and advocate for the brand, becoming brand ambassadors. Opportunity Fund recently held an internal brown-bag session titled "How Do You Talk About Opportunity Fund If Anyone Asks You?" for whom the target audience was employees who were not formally involved in communications, such as office managers, loan operations staff, and others. Through role-play exercises, these individuals were given the opportunity to practice articulating what is meaningful to them about the organization's brand. There was no prescribed speech or key message; the session was configured more as an opportunity to learn about the organization, share perceptions and approaches, and determine what resonated most for each individual who attended. This approach recognizes that all staff members have a role to play in communicating the brand and that everyone can become a brand ambassador. Another key effect of these participative sessions is that they lead to an increase in staff motivation and feelings of pride and connection to their organization.

The World Wildlife Fund (WWF) recently engaged staff through an elevator speech contest that asked people how they would describe WWF in thirty seconds. Initially, the plan was to select a winning elevator speech, but as the entries were judged, the importance of personal stories became evident. "One single 'company line' doesn't work . . . it just doesn't ring true," noted Kerry Zobor, vice president of communications at WWF (Jayawickrama, 2011, p. 5). Instead of one winner, three entries were chosen as examples of how personal stories can bring WWF to life.

In the case of Educate Girls, the community volunteers through whom the organization delivers services are also their key brand ambassadors. To support these village-level volunteers, the organization offers frequent training sessions on the organization, its values, and the brand. A help desk provides volunteers with a continuous source of support and a means of answering questions as they arise. When Educate Girls staff initially enter a community, they tend to provide more structured direction and guidance on the brand and the use of the brand. Over time, as volunteers integrate and embody the brand, less direct guidance is required.

The opportunities and range of activities and formats to engage internal stakeholders are plentiful. Although doing so takes time and planning, and sometimes does not feel immediately essential, engaging internal stakeholders can really pay off in terms of brand Integrity, organizational cohesion, and a more motivated and connected group of staff and employees.

Engage External Audiences

Organizations that are achieving brand Democracy also engage external audiences. Part of this takes place through the research phase discussed previously, during which external audiences are asked about their perceptions of the organization, and part of it builds on the increasing dialogue that is possible due to the growth in social media. This gives audiences an opportunity to contribute to defining identity, which can lead to greater engagement and ultimately to these audiences' becoming brand ambassadors. Beneficiaries are an important external stakeholder group, but one that is often neglected in soliciting input, in part because gathering data from beneficiaries can be challenging. Organizations are increasingly designing methods to get the perspective of beneficiaries before, during, and after implementing programs. There are several new initiatives (Keystone Accountability and CDA Collaborative Listening Project are good examples) that are gathering beneficiary feedback for organizations. Soliciting feedback is certainly one way to create more engagement with this audience (Twersky, Buchanan, and Threlfall, 2013).

Organizations that have strong brands also encourage external stakeholders to advocate on their behalf. According to Matt Wells, executive director at Diavolo Dance Theater, "Social media has really changed the game. We used to be really protective about our brand. Now, every time we have a performance, photos and videos end up all over YouTube, Facebook, and Twitter. Now we embrace this as a strength to build our supporters. This works much better than squelching their enthusiasm, since the world is already trending so strongly toward sharing." Organizations need to change their mindset to embrace the new brand paradigm in which external stakeholders are actively engaged in defining and communicating the brand. Exploring and experimenting with all kinds and forms of social media are vital for nonprofits. These activities should be driven specifically by the goals of engaging a spectrum of external stakeholders and creating brand ambassadors. Social media is both a driver of brand Democracy and one of the key tools to implement it.

By defining key stakeholder segments and engaging them through the social media of their choice and preference, you can create two-way communications that are the basis for deeper engagement and participation in the brand. Invite your supporters to post stories, photos, and suggestions to your organizational website. This creates a channel for external stakeholders, particularly younger audiences, to provide key content to your site and participate in building the brand identity. By sharing something of themselves, external stakeholders build a sense of relationship and emotional connection with your organization and its brand. Beth Thoren, director of communications and fundraising at the Royal Society for the Protection of Birds, is inviting supporters who know about gardening techniques that will protect wildlife to share their stories with others, thereby engaging them and advancing the organization's mission at the same time.

In *The Dragonfly Effect*, Jennifer Aaker and Andy Smith (2010) discuss how to use social media effectively through tapping into people's emotions. The four "wings" of the dragonfly include focus, or identifying a single clear goal; grabbing attention through simple, visual means; engaging and using stories (which we discuss in a later section); and taking action. When you have a clear goal for your communication and you offer an opportunity to connect through stories or action, then you can build valuable relationships with your audiences.

Decentralize Responsibility for Brand Communications

When internal stakeholders participate in the process of defining the brand and begin to talk about the brand in a personal, authentic, and meaningful way, then strict controls are not necessary. Using a brand Democracy approach based on education, engagement, and the provision of tools is an alternative to brand policing and control. The organizations we talked with are moving increasingly toward decentralizing responsibility for brand communications and providing guidance, templates, and tools rather than a set of fixed rules and communication products that require policing. We described earlier the extensive effort that YMCA Canada undertook to build brand Integrity and brand Democracy. Despite the positive reception to its efforts and the engagement of YMCA Canada member organizations, Meghan Reddick acknowledged that tensions remained in the organization between the desire to focus on local community needs and the need for a common brand positioning and identity. One way in which YMCA Canada has addressed this tension is by providing templates and materials to member organizations to support the brand effort. "We save member organizations a lot of time and money by providing them with tools and templates from which they can choose to reflect their local community needs. We also have provided detailed brand guidelines and recommendations, and a photo bank they can use."

Many other organizations are also using this approach. Bev Schwartz, vice president of global marketing at Ashoka, has developed a number of communication tools that reside in an internal resource center for use by Ashoka staff around the world. She explains that rather than requiring internal stakeholders to use specific materials and trying to control everything that goes out, her approach is to create valuable tools that in and of themselves serve as guidelines and parameters. She explained, "Instead of saying, 'These are the templates I want you to use,' I say, 'Here are some templates that you can edit, use what you need, add your own text, change the photos, etc.'" Schwartz goes on to explain that everything Ashoka develops is a "templatable" tool, modular, flexible, and global, and that she encourages flexibility around adoption of those templates, "so people could be a little different, but still belong to the same brand family." She concluded that "everybody started to appreciate the idea. It made their life easier, and they started to see the utility in the uniformity of the materials worldwide. Using similar graphics and language to describe Ashoka made for a more sophisticated and united organizational appearance. As a result, satisfaction developed internally, and the resource center, with all its flexible templates, was deemed a success."

By supplying templates that are easy to use and customize, you can facilitate the implementation of a new or revised brand and increase brand consistency across the organization. Providing useful templates and materials that stakeholders will want to use and can easily adopt is an effective alternative to policing brand communications. When you use a guiding rather than controlling approach with adaptable tools, you gain flexibility and address the fundamental shift in the nature of communications that we have discussed. In order for this aspect of brand Democracy to work, however, you must have a clear brand identity.

Laura Sanchez noted that Living Cities created communications guidelines for tweeting and blogging and established an internal working group called "the Presence Team" to help deconstruct what they do, problem-solve, foster internal clarity, and provide training and coaching internally. BRAC's work on aligning its brand with its core values enabled the organization to focus on training people on the principles of the brand, setting boundaries, and providing guidelines rather than creating a bureaucratic approval process for every communication.

For organizations that operate in varying regions and cultures, flexibility in tailoring communications to local audiences is especially important. Some organizations have focused on communicating a guiding idea rather than a specific message or tagline. For example, when Special Olympics realigned its brand, it provided an illustration in words and pictures. The visual representation helped ensure that people of varying cultures, languages, and literacy levels could all understand this guiding idea that was the core of the brand. HelpAge International also recently rebranded, but did not insist on strict consistency in external communications. Affiliates use variations of the same logo, with text that is customized to the local population. "Communicating ideas rather than words, fonts, or colors is less likely to get lost in translation," explained Mayur Paul.

The brand Democracy approach to managing the brand using guidelines, templates, and support tools is also easier and less expensive to implement and can unleash creativity and innovation within the organization. At United Way, Cynthia Round described how the organization continues to improve thanks to the interaction among its members. Many creative ideas have come up from the network and been shared across the organization. The brand management intranet site offers easy access to brand guidelines, tools, and templates for local adaptation, and an image library. The organization also holds communications contests and showcases local adaptations at their conferences to recognize the best workplace campaign, best website, and best print ad. This helps the nonprofit achieve both "greater consistency and innovation within this consistency," while also contributing to employee pride.

Jennifer Benito-Kowalski from Save the Redwoods League described how a strong brand makes it easier to encourage creativity. She emboldens people in the organization to try new things: "'You know our brand,' I tell them. 'Go for it!'" Implementing brand Democracy and brand Integrity together allows you to encourage more creativity from staff, keeping them engaged and more willing to share ideas and best practices. Providing guidelines and tools is most effective when you have worked on brand Integrity and your staff have internalized a strong understanding of the brand.

An increasing number of organizations are choosing to ensure that their brand image stays consistent by using internal brand handbooks that capture the essence of the brand and describe the brand parameters and guidelines. Amnesty International has created the Little Yellow Book, BRAC has the Magenta book, and Publish What You Pay has developed the "passport." Each of these documents conveys the essence of the brand, typically including something about the history, approach or methods, and values of the organization. At Amnesty, the Little Yellow Book was developed through a brand Democracy approach, and its content is meant not to be memorized but to convey a set of ideas that readers can develop further. The Little Yellow Book is not prescriptive, but rather is intended to encourage creativity. It is not trying to freeze the brand, but instead marks a stage in its continuing development. As Markus Beeko, director of campaigns and communications, explained, "The Little Yellow Book is just another milestone. The brand keeps moving, keeps developing. Amnesty is not an organization where people will make it the Bible. It helps us when we talk to each other and when we talk to our stakeholders, but it is not about the book. It's about a feeling, even if you use different words" (Stone, 2011, p. 5). The Omaha Community Foundation's brand book contains messaging related to the brand, including its positioning, rational words and emotional words that describe the foundation, its tagline, brand narrative, audiences, and look and feel. Only after these concepts have been articulated does the book provide the details of the logo, colors, color palette, photos and illustrations, and typography. The book includes several sample applications.

Although it may at first be hard to switch away from the brand policing mode and decentralize responsibility for communicating the brand, we believe that if you have brand Integrity and support a brand Democracy approach, you can stimulate the emergence of internal brand ambassadors and provide them with the tools and support to articulate the brand in an authentic yet consistent way.

Use Stories

Organizations are increasingly using stories to talk about their brands, both internally and externally. Stories are posted on office walls and on Facebook and are included in annual reports. They can bring to life the experiences of beneficiaries and the passion of founders, donors, volunteers, and staff. Stories can effectively transmit the mission and values of the organization. At Save the Redwoods League, Benito-Kowalski indicated that they have "increasingly focused on stories and the people behind them to connect with all our stakeholders," incorporating them into the brand handbook in recognition that the stories resonate with people internally as well as externally and can be more compelling than bare facts. Jill Taylor, manager of foundation relations at the American Academy of Pediatrics, is coaching staff in storytelling to help people connect more directly with the work of the organization.

Although data can be very helpful in appealing to the "head," stories appeal to the "heart." Stories are powerful in helping people connect emotionally with an organization. Stories about the organization's founding can convey the passion and values that are an important part of the history of the organization. Stories about beneficiaries and program outcomes directly communicate the mission and impact. When you train people to share their own stories, you increase the connection to the brand and promote authenticity and engagement. Tom Kuplic, president of ETO Consulting, suggested,

> We all love stories because they deliver on fundamental emotional needs we all have—whether it is to feel a sense of belonging, achievement, or discovery. Stories of heroes, mentors, caregivers, and explorers have been around in all cultures since we started telling stories around the fire, and still resonate with us today because they help us feel things we want to feel. We call these "archetypal stories," and when nonprofit brands can evoke one of these stories through their actions and messaging, people connect more deeply with their organization because there is a sense of familiarity to the narrative—"I know that story!" They feel they know what to expect from it. Alignment around a single archetypal story also helps guide the organization's staff to act consistent with the brand story.

In describing his position at the Gates Foundation, Tom Scott noted that "I like to say I'm a brand storyteller. My role as it relates to the foundation brand is to help bring the stories of our work to life for the audiences that are important to us." Noah Manduke described two benefits of storytelling. Stories, he said, "help close the proximity gap between issues and those who care about them . . . They are critical for making vivid the gravity of the problem and proximity of the solution. The fact that we really can solve these problems can really rouse people." Second, he noted that "storytelling can be a proxy for branding. In branding, you need to define your unique significance, deliver on that, and dramatize it to different constituents. Storytelling allows work to speak for itself." Finally, storytelling also plays an important role in social media, as a mechanism by which both internal and external stakeholders can become effective brand ambassadors. Table 8.3 summarizes key suggested activities for supporting brand ambassadors by engaging internal and external stakeholders, decentralizing brand communications, and using stories.

CREATE AFFINITY FOR GREATER IMPACT

The principle underlying brand Affinity is that in order to implement their mission and maximize impact, organizations cannot operate in

TABLE 8.3. *Support Brand Ambassadors*

What to Do	How to Do It	Tools and Tactics
Engage internal stakeholders	• Create training and education sessions • Build participative approaches to discussing brand identity	• Use the paradigm shift to address skeptics • Develop a training plan and programs on the subject of brand for your staff • Establish core teams, councils, and brand leads to broaden the engagement of stakeholders • Use all kinds of meetings, conferences, and retreats for staff and volunteers to share their thoughts and ideas on your organization's brand identity

(Continued)

TABLE 8.3. *Support Brand Ambassadors (Continued)*

What to Do	How to Do It	Tools and Tactics
Engage external audiences	• Research perceptions of external stakeholders • Use targeted social media to engage and promote the participation of key external stakeholders	• Solicit feedback from external stakeholders, including beneficiaries, about your brand • Use YouTube, Facebook, Twitter, Pinterest, and other forums to engage discussions and share content with specific external stakeholder segments • Invite supporters to post and share content (photos, stories, advice) on your site to create connection and engagement
Decentralize responsibility for brand communications	• Develop brand guidelines, templates, and tools and allow some flexibility	• Establish an intranet site with a variety of communication templates, photo banks, and recommendations and frameworks • Create a brand handbook • Promote sharing of communications best practices across your organization
Use stories	• Promote the use and sharing of stories to support brand ambassadors	• Train staff in how to capture and share stories using multiple media (videos, photos, interviews, case studies) • Solicit stories from all stakeholders (beneficiaries, volunteers, staff, donors, board members) to convey mission, values, and passion for your organization • Be creative in where and how you share stories both internally and externally, using traditional and social media and integrating them into all communications

isolation. Affinity refers to using the brand in partnerships to achieve shared social impact. The work organizations do to strengthen their brand by implementing brand Integrity through brand Democracy is important groundwork for achieving brand Affinity. In this section, we propose three specific sets of activities and actions to implement brand Affinity: staying tuned in to sector changes and engaging other organizations; articulating and advocating shared goals and promoting partner brands; and using open-source platforms and sharing tools and brand assets.

Stay Tuned In to Sector Changes and Engage Other Organizations

As we described in the previous chapter on brand Affinity, the first step to implementing brand Affinity is to gain clarity on one's own brand identity, values and goals, and theory of change. How to accomplish this has largely been articulated in the previous sections on achieving brand Integrity through brand Democracy. We have discussed how defining an organization's positioning and differentiation relative to other players is a fundamental precursor both to defining brand identity and to identifying partners that can help achieve broader mission impact. Articulating the organization's theory of change also enables nonprofits to identify specific gaps that need to be filled by potential partners.

In order to build brand Affinity, an organization also needs to understand its ecosystem, the trends and forces shaping that ecosystem, and the key actors and players. Funders as well as the other players themselves are often a good source of information. Organizing an information-sharing or networking event can help shed light on what different players are doing and thinking, which will also help build possible collaborations. Sasha Chanoff of RefugePoint is passionate about the importance of sector collaboration and partnerships and is actively engaged in Refugee Council USA, a coalition of organizations welcoming and protecting refugees. "We are focused on expanding support and efforts for refugees, and collaborations play a key role in this," he stressed. "Understanding the role that other organizations in this area play helps crystallize our own role and enables us collectively to move the agenda for vulnerable refugees."

Steve Mendez, director of marketing at United Way of Dane County (Wisconsin) has helped pioneer a shift in his organization's approach to community development that demonstrates brand Affinity. "We see ourselves as community conveners," he explained. "We use the United

Way brand and the trust it carries to bring together partners from different fields that can help address a particular issue in the community." This community impact model coordinates the efforts of multiple partners by defining specific goals and measurements and by incorporating a clear understanding of the individual role that each partner has in the broader theory of change. Community impact directors from United Way are able to identify and attract the right partners to address specific issues. They bring together issue experts, business partners with financial assets, and community leaders who are critical to successful implementation. "The United Way brand acts like an overarching brand that helps in the whole partnership process," stated Mendez. "By using the brand," he added, "we can bring more resources to bear and align people around a specific set of common goals."

This coordination and convening role requires not only knowledge of the players across sectors who are interested in specific issues (such as education or senior citizen support) but also an understanding of the positioning and unique convening value that the United Way brand can bring to partnerships. In this example, the brand attracts partners and brings validity to the collaborative community efforts. As we have discussed, identifying your unique contribution and reaching out to other organizations that complement or enhance impact from a theory-of-change perspective are key steps in identifying partners and implementing brand Affinity.

A number of our interviewees shared with us that their partnership opportunities arose somewhat haphazardly or emerged from chance encounters and that many of these partnerships did not end up being particularly successful at driving mission impact. You must proactively seek out partners that make sense for your organization, given your positioning, theory of change, and unique value contribution. A clear brand identity will help determine and attract quality partnership opportunities.

Articulate and Advocate Shared Goals and Promote Partner Brands

Our research indicates that when organizations are focused on shared external goals or a common cause, collaborations and partnerships become more productive. Shereen Tyrrell, former director of public education for the Massachusetts Children's Trust Fund, described how the focus on a shared cause helped overcome concerns about organizations that are otherwise competing for the same funding streams. "We can differentiate ourselves from our competitors because we play a different role, but in the end we are all working toward preventing child abuse," she explained. "When there's a large funding stream," she added, "it makes it easier to collaborate, but we are ultimately about trying to promote the work that our 'competitors' do as well, so even though we're competing, we're still happy if they do well fundraising because we have the same goals." The focus on a shared goal can attract partners and create the context for developing collaboration and brand Affinity.

One of the attributes of brand Affinity is the ability to share credit and promote partner brands such that social impact overall is maximized. SumOfUs.org describes itself as "a global movement of consumers, investors, and workers all around the world, standing together to hold corporations accountable for their actions." It relies on partnerships to achieve impact and strives to position itself as a partner of choice with other online organizers. According to Taren Stinebrickner-Kaufman, executive director and founder, when the organization achieves a campaign success, it deliberately avoids claiming sole credit for victory. Rather, it recognizes members for their actions and acknowledges the importance of broad coalitions in effecting change. SumOfUs .org understands that even though this does not maximize its own brand's potential visibility, it helps maintain a positive and constructive relationship with partners, encouraging coordination and the sharing of resources and information that in turn results in greater shared impact.

Promoting the visibility of partner brands not only increases your overall impact but also strengthens your image as a valuable partner. This notion of becoming a partner of choice was echoed by many of our interviewees; demonstrating a "partnership mentality" and the ability to successfully manage partnerships helps attract additional partners. As Lesley Fuller, funding, marketing, and communications manager at Kibble Education and Care Centre based in Paisley, Scotland, commented, "The growth in partnerships—with staff at all levels across the organization working collaboratively with other organizations and being invited to join networks, sit on various committees, and take up directorships on other charitable or social enterprise boards—has been one of the key shifts in Kibble's experience over the past ten years." Whereas Kibble's brand used to be perceived in somewhat negative terms as a "closed institution," with little public understanding of what Kibble actually did (youngsters were warned, "If you don't behave, you'll be sent to the Kibble"), the nonprofit is now frequently sought out for partnerships by many organizations, including universities, researchers, and local community groups. Fuller believes that this is in part due to the organization's clear niche, local footprint, and community roots, and because it has demonstrated value as a local partner. Demonstrating value, which flows back to building brand equity and implementing mission, is important for brand Affinity to work. Facts and data that validate the benefits of partnership can help you overcome concerns about working with partners that some within your organization might consider to be competitors.

In the case of Lincoln Center, having data on the behaviors of constituents enabled partners to develop and buy into a common strategy to serve these constituents. Lincoln Center is emulating an approach being used in Philadelphia where customer research on patrons of the arts is helping to drive collaborations with other arts nonprofits. Not only can data be used to promote brand Affinity, but much can be learned from studying the successes and failures of other organizations, as a form of historical data. In Lincoln Center's case, Peter Duffin is spearheading a brand Affinity approach in New York that is already working in Philadelphia. Comparative and best practice data can be very useful for organizations looking to build and manage their brands using tried and tested approaches.

Jack Sim of the World Toilet Organization has built his organization by focusing on partnerships and identifying how he can leverage other organizations' assets and expertise. He views everyone as a potential partner and is particularly tuned in to the value that his organization brings to those partnerships he cultivates. "For example, I give journalists a good story about shit in a way that's interesting and funny. The journalists give me media coverage and prominence to the work. So if a politician stands next to me, they also get positive media coverage and legitimacy, and then in turn they can help other NGOs and our partners in the field." Being cognizant of partners' needs and wants allows you to creatively and effectively create value for a variety of partners, often at little or no cost.

Use Open-Source Platforms and Share Tools and Assets

Nonprofit brands and their organizations can benefit tremendously from the power of Internet-based platforms and the growth in social media and open innovation. Movement brands, such as the Girl Effect, in particular have been able to successfully tap into social media to drive awareness and support. Those organizations that have been most successful have used open-source platforms and various forms of crowdsourcing to extend the boundaries of their organization and catalyze awareness and support for their organization and social mission. The notion of "ownership" of the brand and brand assets is fundamentally different for these organizations; success is measured by how widely and broadly brand assets are being adopted and shared by both supporters and partner organizations.

Will Novy-Hildesley calls this phenomenon "Bigger Than [You]" and noted that these brands extend beyond their organizational boundaries and display what he called "brand generosity." Making brand assets and tools (videos, photos, stories, data, and templates) available to partners creates transparency and trust, which promotes collaboration and drives impact. Our recommendation is therefore to consider making brand assets and tools available to partners with the objective of advancing shared goals. In brand Democracy, we advocate sharing templates and tools internally. Brand Affinity extends this same approach for external partners.

Just as the roles of donors and beneficiaries are changing with the increasing porosity of organizational boundaries and open innovation, so too is the role that partners can play in achieving mission implementation. By thinking of partners and supporters as team members, and freeing activities from traditional organizational boundary constraints, Free Lunch for Children, a nonprofit in China, exploded into a national phenomenon. In its first eight months of operation, this nonprofit, run by volunteers and supported in part by the government-owned China Social Welfare Foundation, has raised nearly $3 million from sixty thousand donors, provided free lunches for fifteen thousand children on an ongoing basis, and catalyzed changes in government programs that are attempting to replicate the model. Transparency and openness are key organizational values espoused by its founder, Deng Fei (a well-known Chinese journalist), and all organizational data are widely available and published on Weibo (the Chinese equivalent of Twitter). Each participating partner school has a Weibo account where procurement, menus, and the number of children served is published every day. In a recent media interview, Deng explained, "As an experienced investigative journalist, I know that information transparency is a lifeline. This is also my personal principle. Free Lunch publishes all cash flow data, and we welcome Weibo users' supervision of our activities." Weibo is a platform that empowers partners and supporters to get directly involved through donations, spreading the message, and tracking program implementation. Everyone can become part of the success of this movement, which provides individuals with the experience of participation and control, both still uncommon in China. Using open-source platforms can allow you to further your shared goals and build broad support for your social objectives. Table 8.4 summarizes key suggested activities for creating brand Affinity by staying tuned in to sector changes and engaging other

TABLE 8.4. *Create Affinity for Impact*

What to Do	How to Do It	Tools and Tactics
Stay tuned in to sector changes and engage other organizations	• Seek out opportunities to share information and learn about the sector dynamics and key players • Be proactive rather than reactive in reaching out to potential partners	• Reach out to funders to tap into their knowledge of players and forces shaping the ecosystem • Convene information-sharing sessions with other organizations in your sector • Join coalitions and industry groups • Play coordinating and convening roles where possible • Develop criteria for potential partnerships based on an understanding of mission and theory of change
Articulate and advocate shared goals and promote partner brands	• Define and promote common goals and shared social visions or theories of change • Promote the visibility of partner brands and shared issues	• Focus on shared common external goals in discussions with other players • Share space, visibility, and credit for success with other players • Become a partner of choice by adding value in creative, low-cost ways • Use data and facts to provide proof of value and gain partnership buy-in
Use open-source platforms and share brand assets and tools widely with partners	• Build open-source platforms that engage partners in developing and using brand tools and assets • Make brand tools and assets widely and freely available	• Develop videos, photos, fact sheets, posters, and stories that can be used by partners to support common social goals • Ask partners to share their tools and participate in the development of shared resources and activities

organizations, articulating and promoting shared goals, and using open-source platforms.

MEASURING THE IMPACT OF BRANDING ACTIVITIES AND RETURN ON BRAND INVESTMENT

We are sometimes asked how an organization can measure the success of their brand or branding project, or the return on investment of the time and resources needed to manage the brand. When brand is viewed primarily as a fundraising tool, the resulting increase in donations or fundraising impact is a popular measurement to use. Organizations that attempt to measure brand value typically use a discounted flow of future expected fundraising dollars. We believe that this restricted view of brand value and this limited measure are insufficient. Harris Poll EquiTrend measures brand health rather than brand value, using such measures as consumer awareness, how positively consumers think of the brand, and their likelihood of donating to a brand. Although more nuanced, the measure still equates brand health with the ability to fundraise. Both the brand value and brand health measures fail to capture the much broader and more strategic role that a nonprofit brand plays, and they are based on the old view of brand rather than the new brand paradigm.

The idea of having a single metric to evaluate brand impact and strength is alluring. But given the complex and strategic role that brands play in attracting partners, building internal cohesion, and driving social impact in nonprofit organizations, such a metric is unlikely to be useful or relevant. Just as it is difficult to measure the ROI for developing a strategy or for a strategic planning process, it is also difficult to measure the ROI of branding. Instead, we propose using the Role of Brand Cycle described in Chapter Four as a tool to help assess the impact that a brand has on the ability of the organization to implement its mission. Specifically, we suggest that you measure both organizational cohesion and external trust as fundamental precursors to the ability of your organization to effectively and efficiently implement its mission and as indicators of a strong brand. We recognize that organizational cohesion and external trust are not simply the result of a strong brand and that other important factors, such as individual leadership and specific context, play important roles. However, strong brands that strive for brand Integrity, are built through brand Democracy, and promote brand Affinity will contribute, as we have argued, to cohesion and trust.

The Role of Brand Cycle (illustrated in Figure 4.1) depicts a circular process: brand identity and image (brand Integrity) lead to cohesion and trust, connect to capacity and impact, and loop back to reinforce identity and image. This reinforcement back to enhancing identity and image occurs as your organization executes its mission. People (internal and external) can observe that the organization is doing (or not doing) what it says it does and that it is successfully (or perhaps unsuccessfully) attracting human, financial, and organizational resources and building organizational capacity. Perceptions are formed on the basis of these observations and inform both the internal understanding of the brand identity and its external image. We heard from a number of individuals who said that "our work defines our brand." This holds true when your brand is aligned with your organization's mission and strategy. In this case, the work of your organization ultimately reinforces your brand.

ORGANIZATIONAL COHESION, CAPACITY, AND IMPACT

Organizational cohesion is the main internal benefit or outcome of good brand management. The payoff for investing in building brand Integrity using brand Democracy is a more cohesive organization with greater internal trust, engagement, commitment, and motivation on the part of employees, board members, and volunteers, all of whom are focused and united in their decision making and actions now that the brand provides the "white lines in the road." The result of organizational cohesion is therefore increased organizational effectiveness and efficiency, better decision making, and less mission drift, as well as greater capacity—all of which lead directly to increased impact.

It is interesting to note that the brand, as the embodiment of the mission, helps accomplish the three functions that Sharon Oster (1995) identifies for the mission statement itself. "Mission statements serve boundary functions, act to motivate both staff and donors, and help in the process of evaluation of the organization" (p. 22). The process of building brand Integrity through brand Democracy can guide operational decision making by the board and staff (boundary function), can motivate and attract both internal and external stakeholders (motivational function), and becomes an element in the evaluation of organizational success (evaluation function).

Public Education Foundation provides an example of building cohesion through the branding process. Staff redefined brand identity, connected it with the organization's mission and values, and aligned it with the external image, redesigning their website and becoming more proactive in encouraging people to act as brand ambassadors. In addition to gaining clarity in terms of their brand, the branding process itself has had an impact on the internal capacity and cohesion of the organization. "Using the brand IDEA framework and process have really created organizational cohesion for us," emphasized Christa Payne. "Many more of us now understand the value of communication and people now feel they have a part and a role to play. Talking about the brand becomes everyone's responsibility because everyone helped build it." The following are some possible relevant metrics you might use to track organizational cohesion as an outcome of effective brand management:

- A sense of all pulling together

- Level of professional and personal engagement

- Alignment of decision making

- Perceived effectiveness of both the individual and organization

- Perceived changes in organizational capacity to implement the mission

Exhibit 8.1 outlines a brief questionnaire or survey that could be used to track these metrics for three key internal audiences: board members, staff, and volunteers. Your own organization will of course be able to develop a more relevant and customized set of survey questions for your specific situation; ensuring anonymity will increase the validity of the resulting data. Starting with some specific questions and then ending with a few open-ended ones might work well both to track changes over time and to uncover new issues for your organization. The following questionnaire could be administered at regular intervals to assess the impact of specific branding activities on your organization's cohesion.

EXTERNAL TRUST

Trust stems from being who you say you are and is the main external outcome of good brand management. A clear brand positioning, focused brand image, and strong brand Integrity all build trust. The result of your investing in building brand Integrity using brand Democracy and promoting brand Affinity is enhanced trust in the organization on the part of beneficiaries, donors, and partners of all kinds. Engaging stakeholders means connecting with them at a personal and emotional level and building relationships, which are the foundations of trust. The trust of external audiences is what drives the ability of your organization to build capacity through attracting financial and human resources and building relationships. Trust on the part of beneficiaries is important if your organization is to implement your programs effectively; donor trust

EXHIBIT 8.1.   *Measuring Cohesion and Effectiveness*

Please answer the following questions using a 1–5 scale, where 5 is the maximum.

1. How would you rate the extent to which the members of your organization, including yourself, share a common understanding of the organization's mission and strategy?	1	2	3	4	5
2. To what extent are you and your colleagues working in alignment toward that mission and strategy?	1	2	3	4	5
3. How engaged do you feel in the mission and strategy of the organization?	1	2	3	4	5
4. How engaged do you feel toward the organization itself?	1	2	3	4	5
5. How easy is it for you to make professional decisions?	1	2	3	4	5
6. To what extent is your organization effective?	1	2	3	4	5

Please answer the following questions in a few sentences.

Has your organization increased its ability to implement the mission and achieve impact? Why or why not?	
In what ways do you feel that your organization is more or less cohesive than before?	
How might your organization be more effective at implementing its mission and achieving impact?	

is essential for those who cannot themselves judge the organization's services; and partner trust is key for collaborative engagements. So here again we have three audiences to whom a survey or series of questionnaires can be administered. These tools focus on measures of trust and can include other aspects important to each of the constituents. Exhibit 8.2 outlines a brief sample survey that could be adapted by your organization.

EXHIBIT 8.2. *Measuring External Trust and Capacity*

Please answer the following questions using a 1–5 scale, where 5 is the maximum.

1. How would you rate the extent to which you trust organization X to do what it says?	1	2	3	4	5
2. To what extent do you trust organization X to carry out its work efficiently?	1	2	3	4	5
3. To what extent do you believe that organization X conducts itself in accordance with its values?	1	2	3	4	5
4. To what extent do you feel that organization X is responsive to your needs?	1	2	3	4	5
5. To what extent is organization X your first choice in its field of activity?	1	2	3	4	5
6. How effective is organization X in implementing its mission?	1	2	3	4	5
7. How efficient is organization X in conducting its work?	1	2	3	4	5

Please answer the following question in a few sentences.

What should organization X do to increase your trust in it?	

It is important to stress that these are simply examples of potential survey questions and should be modified to meet the unique needs and circumstances of your organization. Also, we believe that opportunities exist every day for you to collect informal, qualitative information on the attitudes and beliefs of both internal and external stakeholders with regard to cohesion and trust. And as we mentioned earlier, it is important to track these metrics over time to evaluate the impact of new and sustained branding initiatives.

SUMMARY

Many nonprofit organizations believe that it is difficult and costly to build and manage their brands. We believe that brand management is possible for every organization. It is less about creating a cool new logo or costly advertising campaign and more about developing a shared internal brand identity, building brand Integrity through brand Democracy, and using brand Affinity to maximize impact. This chapter suggested some guidelines and specific tactics for achieving this, which begins with a shift in mindset and perspective on what a brand is and can do for the organization. Building brand Integrity through brand Democracy is time consuming and requires patience and perseverance, but the value lies as much in the process, which itself builds organizational cohesion and external trust, as in the final product: a focused brand identity and increased brand Integrity. Broad participation and ongoing education are key components of this process. Building brand Affinity is more than just creating partnerships; it also reflects a new mindset that requires a deep understanding of the ecosystem, establishing and focusing on shared goals, promoting and adding value to others, and sharing brand assets to maximize social impact.

CHAPTER

THE BRAND IDEA IN SPECIFIC SITUATIONS

In the previous chapter, we discussed how to implement the brand IDEA and provided some specific suggestions for activities and tools to help nonprofits implement brand Integrity through brand Democracy and create brand Affinity for greater impact. We also briefly introduced an approach for measuring the impact or return on investment of brand efforts. In this chapter, we turn to an analysis of the brand IDEA in specific situations, across different types of organizations, and at different points in an organization's life cycle.

BRAND MANAGEMENT IN DIFFERENT SITUATIONS

The brand IDEA framework is applicable to all nonprofit organizations regardless of their size, maturity, or area of focus. In this section, we explore some of the more typical brand management challenges that nonprofit organizations typically encounter and describe the role that brand Integrity, Democracy, and Affinity can play.

Brand Building

For new organizations and start-ups, the brand is built concurrently with the organization. As the mission, values, and strategy are defined and fine-tuned, so is the brand. To some extent, brand building undertaken as part of establishing and building an organization is the easiest of the brand management challenges we encountered. Alignment is built in from the start, and those nascent organizations that embrace participative engagement of stakeholders in many aspects of their work will naturally extend this engagement to brand building as well.

For many existing organizations, however, issues of brand and brand management have not traditionally been a priority, particularly if the brand had until recently been seen primarily as a fundraising tool. A number of organizations we talked with remain somewhat skeptical about the benefits and usefulness of brand management for their organizations, whereas others are intuitively managing their brands without using the language or frameworks of brand management. Some of these organizations are perhaps just starting to think about how to integrate brand management and brand-building activities into their strategy and operational decision making, and may need to focus first on internal branding and some education around brands.

The Swami Vivekananda Youth Movement (SVYM) is an organization that increasingly has adopted brand management approaches as the organization has grown. The organization's development work in India draws its inspiration from the life and values of Swami Vivekananda. Initially, Dr. Balasubramaniam noted that the brand developed organically as the organization focused on implementing its mission. Over time, he increasingly has incorporated brand management approaches to intentionally building the brand, emphasizing the values of the organization. "For me, brand building is about the concept, the philosophy of development, partnership, Vivekananda and his values." Balasubramaniam is focused on instilling these values through the organizational culture and reflecting them in the brand identity. He also is starting to recognize that "the brand does not operate in isolation; it deals with the entire ecosystem," and that internal alignment needs to take into account the external environment and stakeholders. Regular meetings and retreats help ensure that "employees are constantly reminded of what we do and why we do it." In order to support its goal of sustainable development, the organization is working toward greater brand Democracy by engaging and empowering stakeholders directly to create "true community-based development, where things happen in the community that are actually designed and developed by the community." This approach requires working with others. "Development is not something you can do alone," he emphasized. "My model is not about SVYM; it's about people taking care of themselves and a very empowered state of mind. . . . The more the merrier is our philosophy." Balasubramaniam is also starting to implement aspects of brand Affinity. "Until you recognize that partnership is necessary, you can't really impact the nation and its development," he concluded, and "that means you've got to take your brand to all these people." His conscious and multifaceted approach to brand building is consistent with our brand IDEA framework.

Rebranding

Brand management is a constant process that must be adapted as the environment changes and organizations evolve. For many organizations, a rebranding or branding initiative becomes necessary when the brand identity and brand image are no longer aligned, resulting in weak brand Integrity. This is often the case for nonprofit organizations whose programs and operations have evolved over time but whose brand image remains linked to initial or historic perceptions of the organization.

In 2012, Girl Scouts USA (GSUSA) turned one hundred and undertook an extensive rebranding to try to revitalize the brand and maintain relevance. The effort was based on extensive market research that revealed a disconnect between the internal values of the brand (identity) and the core customers' perceptions of the brand (image), which could be summarized as "camping and cookies." Sharon Lee Thony, director of marketing for GSUSA, explained that "while the mission has remained intact [to build girls of courage, confidence, and character to make the world a better place], the strategies and programs to achieve that mission have evolved with the changing context and environment." Thony believes that the success of the recent rebranding efforts stems from staying true to the mission and core values of the organization, and using external data to guide changes and build support internally for the rebranding process. "When we rebranded and created a new identity, we stayed true to green, the trefoil as an icon, and our mission statement as the three core elements of the brand identity, the same elements that have existed in the Girl Scouts' branding since 1912. We also emphasized that the changes we were making were a direct result of the consumer insights and changing needs of girls today, and this enabled us to get buy-in for the rebranding effort internally."

As programs and operations change, the organization's key audiences and issues can change as well, and this can also reduce alignment between identity and image. This was the case at Save the Redwoods League, where a rebranding effort was initiated when the organization recognized that the key issues and audiences had both evolved. Jennifer Benito-Kowalski explained, "Leaders recognized that we needed to do something to relate to the next generation of redwood ambassadors, because the average age of our donor was about sixty-seven years old . . . We decided to rebrand the organization to make it more relevant to the next generation and to the changing demographics of California." The organization's challenges had also shifted; they were no longer dealing with logging companies but with climate change, requiring a shift in both strategy and brand identity.

The scope of the rebranding initiative depends on the extent of the lack of alignment between the brand identity and the mission and strategy, on the one hand, and between the brand identity and brand image, on the other. In some cases, the process can be extensive and comprehensive, involving a wide representation of stakeholders and taking months, if not years, to complete. In other cases, the brand might need just to be tweaked to maintain alignment and relevance.

Changing Brand Name

Sometimes, as part of brand building or rebranding initiatives, organizations are confronted with the decision of whether or not to change their brand name. Educators for Social Responsibility, for example, recently recognized the need for the organization to rebrand and decided that as part of the rebranding effort, it also needed to change its name. The main issue was the brand image confusion that existed externally because of its rather misleading name. Jill Davidson, director of publications and communications, remarked that "our name is a real obstacle because it's not accurate and does not reflect what we do. People make mistaken assumptions based on the name and associate us with anti-bullying initiatives, for example. But we care about a much broader array of outcomes, including academic success."

We spoke with several nonprofits that face a situation similar to the one facing Educators for Social Responsibility, where the organization's name does not accurately reflect the organization's mission, or may conflict with the desired brand image. There are also many nonprofits that are known only by an acronym, which gives no indication of the work the organization does or of what its mission is. There are trade-offs, of course, between adopting a new name that is truly reflective of the organization and its mission (and that therefore helps in building brand Integrity) and holding on to a name that imparts no information or causes confusion but that has, over time, gained recognition and built brand equity with certain stakeholders. Although we acknowledge that the effort will require work and can cause more than a little resistance, we nevertheless believe that if a brand name is actually hindering the development of new relationships, either because it is meaningless or it contributes to a mistaken image, it might be time to consider changing it.

The decision to change brand names can elicit a lot of reaction and reticence both internally and externally, but it is a wonderful opportunity to talk about the organization's mission, work, and strategy going forward. The majority of organizations that go through a change in brand name, particularly if they use a brand Democracy approach, stand to reap the benefits of that change through higher brand Integrity and a greater number of new relationships of all kinds. This was certainly the case for RefugePoint, which changed its name from Mapendo in 2010. Sasha Chanoff described the decision and benefits of the name change:

> The name Mapendo was hindering our organization operationally. We are committed to protecting the most vulnerable refugees regardless of ethnicity, nationality, or any other distinguishing characteristic. But, since our earliest efforts focused on rescuing and protecting Congolese refugees, our brand image was as an organization that favored Congolese refugees. This perception of bias was hindering our work and limiting our opportunities to protect the most at-risk refugees. Also, the name Mapendo was harder to remember than an English-language name that might have been more relevant to our work. Our new name, RefugePoint, solved these issues and emanated from discussions with refugees who described our impact on their lives in this way. Various stakeholders now identify quickly with our new name and remember it more easily. At the same time, the perception of bias among operational partners and refugees has disappeared. While there certainly was an emotional investment in our first name, our stakeholders, from refugees to board members, staff, partners, and donors, all favor the new name.

Names can help tell a story and link the organizational image to the identity and ultimately to the mission and values of the organization. We want to caution, however, that names are best when they are short and memorable; they are not intended to convey the full essence of the brand.

Managing Sub-Brands

Occasionally, an organization may have more than one brand to manage. This can happen in an organic way, with sub-brands emerging alongside new programs, or it can happen in a very deliberate manner, with a new brand being built to address a specific group of stakeholders, for example. Indeed, it is most likely to happen in decentralized organizations that are trying to be responsive to local needs and conditions. The Non-Profit Incubator (NPI) in China has been involved in the launch of over one hundred nonprofits and social enterprises. NPI has eight different sub-brands, representing services working to support and build the capacity of nonprofit organizations in China, including consulting, community service, fundraising, and venture fund platforms, and each platform has its own brand and logo. "There are tensions between the platform brands and the NPI brand. We need to understand how best the brands can work together," explained Li Ding.

Maintaining a link to the organizational brand can be difficult when sub-brands have developed their own identity and have established brand equity. When the reputation eclipses the parent brand, however, the organization loses out on potential benefits and synergies that can come from having a sub-brand in the first place. Breakthrough is a human rights organization with multiple successful campaigns that have achieved brand recognition above and beyond that of the Breakthrough brand itself. The leadership realized that Breakthrough wasn't effectively leveraging the success of the various campaigns, as they were not always linked to the organizational brand. Mallika Dutt explained what they did: "To address these challenges, we decided to undertake a brand identity process for Breakthrough itself. We are working to build internal understanding that building our organizational brand identity—and making sure all of our campaigns align with it—is important. We've experienced a mind shift, focusing more on our methodology and approach, not just our issues and end goals. Our identity is about who we are, how we think, and our methodology for our work, which we want to share with other organizations." Although it can be challenging to take a step back and perhaps lose some of the momentum of a strong sub-brand, we believe that maintaining a strong organizational brand is an important objective of brand management. Breakthrough chose to focus on its approach and methodology as a unifying theme for its organizational brand.

Sub-brands should support the overall organizational brand and be connected to it in such a way that they contribute to building the strength of that organizational brand. Too often we observe that sub-brands or dual brands cause confusion among stakeholders and lead to more siloed organizational structures that lack the cohesion and ability to focus on a common mission and drive impact. Although we understand the desire to craft a brand for a new program or for a specific audience, we believe that wherever possible, nonprofit organizations should use a single strong brand, which will be much more effective in helping them maximize impact.

Campaign and Movement Brands

As we have argued in earlier chapters, everything has a brand, including campaigns, causes, and movements. We are sometimes asked, "What is the difference between a brand and a cause, a campaign, or a movement?" In this book, we have focused our discussion on organizational brands and brand management. Here we touch on the relationship between an organizational brand and brands associated with campaigns, causes, and movements. We believe that in the case of campaigns, the time frame is short, and the goals are focused on creating a particular image, raising awareness, or stimulating a particular action. Although a campaign may rely on and use an organization's brand, it reflects this organizational brand more than it defines it. For a cause, which typically has a longer time frame and broader objectives, this is not typically the case. Indeed, for for-profit companies increasingly engaged in cause marketing efforts, the expectation is that the cause brand will positively reflect on the company's brand, whose perception by key audiences is enhanced by the association. Nonprofit organizations whose brands are highly visible and powerful often are able to closely tie their organizational brand to a particular cause, such that the organization represents the cause, and the cause brand and organizational brand become practically synonymous. Amnesty International, Red Cross, and WWF come to mind as examples. The brand IDEA, particularly brand Affinity, can play an important role in the management of campaign and cause brands, but we believe that it is in the creation and management of movement brands that brand Affinity becomes essential.

There is currently tremendous interest and excitement around the growth in movements and the potential ability of movements to create social change. Some authors suggest that changes in information and communication technologies have enabled people to organize themselves without the formal structures of traditional organizations and that now "there is competition to traditional institutional forms for getting things done" (Shirkey, 2008, p. 22). Shirkey suggests that movements are in direct competition with nonprofits and are better able to address social issues, resulting in the potential demise of nonprofit organizations altogether. Others, however, believe that nonprofit organizations can tap into this growing movement phenomenon and participate in, and even drive, movement building. In his book, Darell Hammond (2011) describes one example of a growing number of nonprofit organizations that are turning a "mission into a movement" (p. 154).

In his recent article in the *Stanford Social Innovation Review*, Peter Manzo reviews Scott Goodson's book *Uprising: How to Build a Brand*

and Change the World by Sparking Cultural Movements, and concludes that the most compelling examples of movement marketing (connecting to people by tapping into what they believe and care about) that are provided in the book are examples of nonprofits and social enterprises for which "the cause, the movement itself is the brand" (p. 16). Manzo also suggests that private for-profit companies attempting a similar movement marketing approach through campaigns tend to "lack a movement's shared endeavor," and therefore concludes that in order to be successful, these movements "must appeal to some shared goal as well as to social change" (p. 16). Goodson himself emphasizes the importance of movements' being open and dedicated to sharing, as well as the importance of relinquishing control of the brand and message. These are fundamental aspects of brand Affinity and brand Democracy that we also advocate.

A number of the organizations we interviewed have developed movement brands specifically to engage and attract the participation of a broader number of partners, develop a sense of shared ownership, promote greater collective impact, and expand the reach and impact of the organization that was initially behind the movement brand. It is important to note that creating a movement brand for the explicit purpose of uniting partners under a single banner to further a shared social objective is very different from promoting multiple sub-brands, which, as we have argued, can lead to confusion and brand dilution. The key, as with any brand, is having a clear and well-defined identity and image. In a sense, movement brands are the ultimate expression of brand Affinity—everyone is invited to participate in and drive toward a common external objective under a single banner.

Courtney Tritch, director of marketing at Northeast Indiana Regional Partnership, expanded on the reason for their decision to launch a distinct movement brand. "One of the reasons we launched the Vision 20/20 brand, a program with its own logo and brand, was that we wanted everyone to own it. We wanted to get everyone behind a movement rather than behind an organization. I was nervous about this," she confessed, "but we created a logo that visually connected with our organization's brand and then made the logo and wording accessible to all. We even made it downloadable from the website for everyone to use, which makes it more powerful and more prolific." The expectation in branding a movement is similar to other forms of brand Affinity partnerships—that the collective impact resulting from the movement will be greater than the sum of the impacts of the individual organizations before they participated in the movement.

Bringing together a diversity of actors all united in a single cause can create a power base that is more effective in changing policy (among other things). This was Christian Teriete's experience with TckTckTck, and he noted that "if you can show that something is happening in many places around the world and it's somehow connected and not just some sort of disconnected diverse set of players who don't know about each other and who are not working under the same banner . . . if you can show it's a movement, then you have more power and more impact on your ultimate target audience or decision makers."

Among our interviewees, particularly for smaller and younger organizations, building movements and movement brands was also seen as a way to create a bigger social impact than an individual organization's operating capacity could achieve. "In many ways," explained Xian Zhou of Buy42, "we are trying to change cultural norms surrounding the charity sector in China. We want to empower people to participate in 'doing good' in an easy and natural way that promotes certain values." Forward Greece is another example of a smaller organization that has seen that the work it is doing has had an impact beyond its direct sphere of influence. "The good spillover effect that our movement had was to reactivate a lot of other similar movements," explained Panagiotis Vlachos, who believes that working with these other movements will create an even greater combined impact. "When we promote cooperation, it will be better for everybody—for society and our generation."

When the Nike Foundation spearheaded the development of the Girl Effect movement brand, Emily Brew emphasized the decision to leverage Nike's marketing capabilities and strengths. "We were driven to apply Nike's unique approach to innovation to an issue that stood outside the company's commercial interests," she explained. The foundation did not want to simply write checks; it wanted to realize a much larger impact than a small foundation might typically achieve. "We wanted to be a catalyst to drive demand creation," concluded Brew. "We wanted a lot of people to get on board and create that demand with us" (Kylander, 2011, p. 2). The Nike Foundation certainly achieved this objective and, according to some, has changed the way the field of development addresses teenage girls and their role in alleviating poverty.

Mergers and Acquisitions

The number of mergers and acquisitions in the nonprofit sector will continue to increase, and we believe that the brand IDEA can be a particularly useful framework to help assess these activities. YWCA Boston recently absorbed two smaller nonprofits into its organizational structure. Sylvia Ferrell-Jones, president and CEO, shed light on both of these and the role the brand played. "In the first case," she explained, "the nonprofit was essentially a volunteer organization looking for institutional support. They were drawn to us by the YWCA brand, which they viewed as a strong brand that they felt comfortable with, with significant program alignment with their own activities. In the second case, the nonprofit organization was a separate 501(c)(3), and we essentially acquired their intellectual property. We were intentional and deliberate in this acquisition, which was really a merger, and it went smoothly in part because our two brands were essentially compatible." To some extent, mergers and acquisitions can be considered the ultimate extension of a partnership, and the concept of brand Affinity can be used both to attract potential acquisition targets and to assess the relative fit or overlap of both acquisition and merger candidates. As a merger or acquisition occurs, the concepts of brand Democracy and brand Integrity can help an organization engage stakeholders in redefining and aligning identity and image for the new organization.

BRAND MANAGEMENT FOR DIFFERENT STRUCTURES

The role of brand and the challenges in managing brand can vary depending on the organization's structure and objectives. A single non-profit entity may have an easier time managing brand than a federation, network, or coalition; and a community-based service delivery organization operates in a different brand management context than an online advocacy organization. Although it would be impossible to cover the specific brand management issues of all types of organizational structures and operating strategies, it is possible to make a few general observations on the differences between single-entity nonprofits and those organizations with multiple members or chapters. It is also possible to draw some conclusions about the differences in brand management challenges that service organizations face as opposed to those that confront nonprofits that are more focused on advocacy and policy change.

Nonprofits with Multiple Entities

One of the key challenges facing nonprofit organizations composed of multiple entities, each with varying degrees of autonomy and all sharing the same brand, is ensuring brand Integrity across the organization. For these organizations, brand Democracy becomes an even more important and complex process. Defining and developing a common brand identity that reflects shared values and a communal understanding of the mission is a fundamental starting point that requires skill, time, and commitment to a process of participative engagement. Although single-entity nonprofit organizations need to vertically align key internal stakeholder groups, such as the board members, executives, program directors, staff, and volunteers, nonprofits with multiple entities also need to accomplish horizontal alignment or cohesion across entities—in essence, adding a second dimension to brand Democracy. The larger and more fragmented the organization and the more autonomous the entities, the more daunting this task can appear and the longer it might take to implement brand Democracy. However, the strategies and activities outlined in the previous chapter still apply. The approach undertaken by YMCA Canada was particularly comprehensive and emphasized the importance of education and participative engagement, as well as development of internal champions and cross-functional teams early on, to drive buy-in for both the process and the outcomes.

Local Service Delivery Organizations

For nonprofit organizations that focus on service delivery and have close interactions with their beneficiaries, brand image is essentially a reflection of the staff and volunteers that provide the services and run the programs. Beneficiaries' perceptions of the brand are anchored in how those individuals act, talk, and define the organization. Staff and volunteers *are* the brand in a very real sense. When these organizations have implemented brand Democracy and worked on brand Integrity, then these staff and volunteers are more likely to understand and feel ownership of the brand. Crossover Community Impact (CCI) is a small but powerful development organization with a strong set of values that guide the brand identity, the culture, and the behavior and decision making of staff and volunteers. According to Philip Abode, president of the board, the organization places a strong emphasis on personal relationships, and requests that employees, volunteers, and even board members live in the community that the organization serves. Relocation and living among beneficiaries is a fundamental part of CCI's theory of change. By living the values of the organization, staff and volunteers are trusted to represent the brand; and in the same vein, program development is democratic and driven largely by the grassroots efforts of volunteers and employees.

Advocacy Organizations

For organizations more focused on advocacy and policy change, the brand must help raise awareness of issues; provide compelling evidence; mobilize people, opinions, partnerships, and resources; and create support from a wide variety of collaborators. For these actors, a focus on promoting a shared external goal and the use of open-source brand assets and tools can help engage both internal and external brand ambassadors. Brand Affinity as a brand management approach enables these organizations to build and maintain a variety of partnerships, expand their sphere of influence, and drive policy change.

We have observed that advocacy organizations that are also trying to provide more general education have a particular challenge in managing their brand. When the same brand is used both to convey unbiased information and to advocate for a particular position, external stakeholders may get confused as to what role the organization is playing. This may reflect a lack of brand Integrity when the organization has a dual identity.

Foundations or Grant-Making Organizations

These organizations essentially work through partners to achieve their missions, and must therefore build their brand to attract the right partners and then help those partners shape progress toward a common goal. Brand Affinity is particularly important and relevant for foundations, as is their brand image and maintaining strong brand Integrity, which is often achieved by focusing on organizational values. Increasingly, these organizations are also helping their partners build capacity, brand equity, and effective management of their own brands.

In particular, foundations can play a key role in providing training and capacity building for their partners and in supporting collaborations, not by making it a requirement of funding, but by bringing groups together to share data and identify common goals and related theories of change. This is the approach used by the Silicon Valley Community Foundation, which organizes conferences and networking opportunities for its partners throughout the year.

MANAGING BRANDS AT DIFFERENT STAGES OF THE ORGANIZATIONAL LIFE CYCLE

Organizations, just like people, go through specific stages in their life cycle. Susan Stevens's seminal work (2002) in this area identifies seven stages: idea; start-up; adolescent (growth); mature; decline; turnaround; and terminal. With perhaps the exception of the first and last stages, the brand plays an important role at each stage, although as we shall see, the brand management emphasis is slightly different at each stage. Brothers and Sherman's recent book *Building Nonprofit Capacity* (2011) examines the key managerial challenges and success factors at each stage. We shall use their excellent text as a starting point to discuss the role brand can play in addressing these challenges using the brand IDEA framework. Although all aspects of the brand IDEA are relevant across these growth phases, we have highlighted those aspects that we believe are the most relevant at each stage of the organizational life cycle.

Start-Up Phase

As Brothers and Sherman explain, both new and more seasoned organizations can exist in this phase. They are characterized by a lack of clarity and cohesive internal understanding of the mission, vision, and program strategy. The authors emphasize the importance of clearly articulating the mission, values, and theory of change, as well as the need to develop and nurture trust among internal stakeholders. Some confusion is normal for new organizations that are still trying to define their unique contribution and positioning, but we have also encountered organizations that have been around for decades but whose mission, values, and strategy are at best a little hazy.

In terms of brand management, organizations in the start-up phase need to focus on developing or redeveloping a strong brand identity through a brand Democracy approach and an emphasis on internal branding. Engaging everyone in the process of defining the who, what, and why of the organization will help crystallize and clarify the brand identity, promote discussion about the core or raison d'être of the organization, build trust internally, and achieve widespread buy-in for the brand. Focusing on positioning and differentiation and on making sure that the organization is not duplicating other efforts and can identify its unique value added will also help ensure a clear identity. Achieving brand Integrity will prepare the organization for the growth phase.

Some organizations in this start-up phase, those with weak brand Integrity, are those whose missions are confused or in flux or whose internal constituents disagree about program focus and strategy. In our opinion, a brand Democracy approach to defining brand identity can be of tremendous value for these organizations.

Adolescent (Growth) Phase

In this phase, nonprofits are building management capacity and infrastructure, expanding programs, and developing systems for long-term organizational sustainability. Brothers and Sherman emphasize the need for changes in the board in this phase and the importance of maintaining and refining organizational culture. Organizations in this phase are characterized by constant change and the need to build capacity to support their programs and implement their mission.

In terms of brand management, organizations in the adolescent or growth phase can continue to focus on brand Integrity, with a particular emphasis on brand image and the alignment of brand image with brand identity. The demands surrounding growth in organizational capacity mean that developing trust with external stakeholders through a clear and compelling brand image becomes even more critical. Expanding sources of funding and fundraising relationships, attracting the necessary human resources and expertise, and building influence beyond the organizational boundaries are all supported by a strong, consistent brand image, which increases trust and results in building internal capacity. It is also at this stage that brand increasingly must become a reflection of the organization and its work, rather than being too closely associated with the founder, a particular celebrity, or a powerful partner, which can be the case for organizations in the start-up phase.

The brand IDEA can also be very important in this stage to help prevent mission creep and duplication of existing efforts. Educate Girls is in this growth phase. The nonprofit has developed an effective model that it would like to implement in additional geographical areas throughout India. The effective use of brand Democracy will help Educate Girls generate opportunities, ideas, and enthusiasm via brand ambassadors to support the organization's expansion efforts.

During the growth phase, many organizations are also trying to cross "Moore's chasm" (the gap between early adopters and the majority of customers in high-tech markets) (1999) by building momentum and support to move beyond the initial group of early adopters or supporters. Buy42, the Chinese organization that takes donations of unwanted clothes, resells them online with help from disabled staff, and invests the proceeds back into projects that support people with disabilities, is at just this point. This is a small but successful organization trying to take it to the next level of growth by spurring a movement to change the culture and norms of the charity sector, making charity a part of everyday life in an enjoyable and easy manner. The organization has used social media and Weibo (the Chinese equivalent of Twitter) effectively to achieve this. Brand Democracy and brand Affinity both play important roles at this phase in creating a movement and encouraging the cultural shift required for the organization to grow to the next phase.

Mature Phase

Brothers and Sherman characterize this phase of the life cycle as "impact expansion." These authors suggest that in addition to positioning the organization and using data to support claims, organizations in this phase can "create a bandwagon of meaningful partnerships and community connections which showcase that others believe in your efforts"

(p. 19). Although organizations in this phase are concentrated on expanding their impact, this does not necessarily mean that they do so only through their own organizational growth and program replication; it can also mean expanding support for a particular theory of change or a new idea through other organizations or through policy change.

In terms of brand management, brand Affinity is particularly relevant for mature organizations. The shift in focus from building internal organizational capacity to sharing external goals is at the heart of brand Affinity and, we argue, is the basis for successful partnerships of all kinds. We do not mean to suggest that brand Integrity and brand Democracy are no longer relevant in this phase, or that organizations need to wait until the mature phase to start thinking about brand Affinity. Nevertheless, a focus on brand Affinity can be of particular relevance in the mature phase when organizations seek to expand their impact.

The World Wildlife Fund (WWF) represents a mature organization whose activities have evolved and expanded over time. The challenge for WWF was that for many brand audiences, the well-known panda logo stood only for species conservation and did not convey or reflect their work in land conservation, advocacy, and a myriad of cross-sector partnership efforts. Awareness of the organization was high, but understanding of what it did was low. The organization has worked to clarify mission, strategy, and its brand. As Steve Ertel, director of media and external affairs, described, "We need to do a better job connecting the dots for people . . . we do a good job talking about what we do and how we do it, but we sometimes forget to talk about *why* we do it" (Jayawickrama, 2011, p. 2). The organization works with a broad spectrum of partners to transform markets for specific commodity products, implement field programs, advocate for policy change, and raise awareness and mobilize the public. WWF uses a brand Affinity approach to select partners in each of these areas and uses brand to further these partnerships working toward a greater shared goal. WWF also uses a brand Affinity approach to implement the successful Earth Hour movement, in which people across the world engage in a rolling blackout, switching off their lights for an hour one day every March (Jayawickrama, 2011).

Stagnant Phase

This phase actually incorporates two possible pathways: a period of decline followed by a turnaround or renewal, and a period of decline resulting in dissolution of the organization. In theory, most nonprofit organizations should be working to put themselves out of business in the sense that if they accomplish their mission, they are no longer needed. In practice, this rarely (if ever) happens, and many organizations that enter the stagnant phase attempt a turnaround, with various degrees of success. Typically, turnarounds require both an internal evaluation of the organization's strengths and weaknesses and an external analysis of the threats and opportunities (or SWOT analysis), including an assessment of needs and the current role of other players in the ecosystem. This analysis can then lead to a change in positioning strategy and an update of the brand identity and brand image.

In terms of brand management, the decline or stagnant phase is sometimes characterized by a lack of brand Integrity (described in the earlier section on rebranding) resulting from an older perceived image that has not kept up with the organization's programs and brand identity. In this case, the mission and programs may still be highly relevant, but the perceived brand image is no longer accurate or in line with brand identity. The emphasis should then be on strengthening brand Integrity through a brand Democracy process that engages both internal stakeholders and partners.

In other cases, the fundamental values or mission of the organization may no longer be relevant, and more fundamental changes to the brand identity may be necessary. At this point, the organization may circle back to a start-up phase in terms of brand management, with the additional difficulty of trying to shift away from what may sometimes be a negative brand image. At the United Way of the National Capital Area, Kerry Morgan, senior VP for marketing and communications, described the organization as having spent "ten years trying to be all things to all people, and in the process, ended up being nothing to anyone." The challenge Morgan faced in 2010 was to renew the organization in the wake of both declining revenues and a recent fraud scandal. She and her colleagues set about finding more program focus and revisiting and developing a clear mission and common purpose. Although they encountered resistance to change, Morgan emphasized the importance of using external data to "accelerate the process of creating internal trust" and achieving buy-in for the rebranding initiative.

SUMMARY

Although the starting points and contexts for the specific situations outlined in this chapter differ across varying types of organizations and at diverse points in an organization's life cycle, our recommendations to build brand Integrity through brand Democracy and to drive brand Affinity still apply. We are increasingly seeing nonprofits focus on building or revitalizing their organizational brand in recognition of the important role the brand can play in achieving the mission. Using the brand to engage stakeholders is a key tenet of the brand IDEA and is essential to creating movements. As nonprofits explore mergers and acquisitions, an understanding of brand Affinity can help them select and assess potential opportunities. Although specific brand management issues may differ in emphasis, using the brand IDEA framework can help all organizations identify and address potential issues in order to more effectively achieve their mission and maximize impact.

CONCLUSION
You Can Do It!

This book has articulated a number of important concepts that we hope will help nonprofits, and the people who work with them, manage their brands more effectively and increase their impact. In this conclusion, we attempt to describe what an organization that is successfully implementing the brand IDEA looks like and offer some final recommendations for how individuals in various roles might use the brand IDEA.

USING THE BRAND IDEA

The brand IDEA is a framework to think about brand and a guide for building and managing a brand. We see it as both a diagnostic tool for determining whether an organization is managing its brand effectively and a prescriptive model to guide organizations in their brand management efforts. What we have outlined in the preceding chapters describes each component of the model and how to implement the brand IDEA framework. The principles outlined in Chapter Eight can be helpful in diagnosing potential brand issues for an organization that isn't sure whether or not rebranding is needed. They can be used to test and determine to what extent the organization is following a given principle and to clarify which priorities the organization should choose as it works on more effectively managing its brand. Organizations can also follow these principles and key steps to implement the brand IDEA, whether they are a new start-up or an established organization that is undertaking a rebranding process.

We hope you have been inspired and motivated by the many quotes and examples throughout the text, but we also want to give you some clues as to what an organization does and looks like when it "gets the brand IDEA right." Here is what we have observed in organizations that are successfully managing their brand in line with the brand IDEA framework:

- When an organization has brand Integrity, it anchors brand identity in the mission, values, and strategy to create internal cohesion, meaning that board members, staff, and volunteers fully understand, articulate, and are guided by the "who, what, and why" of the organization. This clarity and shared purpose that lead to organizational cohesion can be important sources of effectiveness and efficiency. An organization with brand Integrity also strives to align identity and image, generating trust with external stakeholders, which in turn enables it to attract resources of all kinds.

- Brand Integrity is a state of being, achieved through the process of brand Democracy. When an organization builds brand Integrity through brand Democracy, internal and external brand ambassadors are empowered and supported. Strict brand controls are replaced by branding guidelines. Organizations implementing a brand Democracy approach recognize that brand is everyone's responsibility and encourage broad participation in the articulation and communication of the brand.

- When an organization uses brand Integrity to drive brand Affinity, it focuses on shared goals and embraces the idea that collaboration maximizes impact. An organization demonstrating brand Affinity uses brand to identify, attract, and add value to partners, and shares credit and brand tools and assets with its partners. Organizations operating with a brand Affinity mindset are focused on expanding the pie, and view partnerships less as an exchange or quid pro quo and more as a strategy for building capacity and driving social change.

USING BRAND IDEA BY FUNCTION

In much the same way that Jennifer McCrea at the Hauser Institute for Civil Society at Harvard University suggests that fundraising is everyone's job, we think that brand management is everyone's responsibility and that a myriad of potential brand ambassadors exist both inside and beyond the organization's boundaries. Key individuals and groups can play an important role in implementing brand Integrity through brand Democracy and promoting a brand Affinity approach. The following section breaks down what we believe are the roles stakeholders can play in building nonprofit brands.

The Role of the Board

Board members are first and foremost brand ambassadors, but they are also the CEO's support team and counselors. Board members can play critical roles in helping shape brand identity, implementing brand Democracy, and championing a brand Affinity approach. A few weeks ago, the board member of a small local nonprofit contacted us for advice on how to go about starting a brand initiative for her organization. Particularly in the case of smaller organizations, board members can often provide the spark and guidance for the organization to start thinking about and investing time and energy in brand management. Board members also are sometimes "canaries in the coal mine" who notice potential mission drift, misalignment, and brand confusion. If you are on the board of a nonprofit, we hope that the brand IDEA gives you a framework for and some guidelines on how to start this process of engagement in order to catalyze change for your organization.

The Role of the CEO

The CEO (or executive director) is the brand steward of his or her organization. Brand stewardship is defined by Karl Speak (1998) as the "active process of managing the brand. Brand stewardship involves a long-term approach to maintaining the brand promise and the brand relationships that create and sustain brand equity" (p. 33). Support for both the brand and brand management activities by the CEO will set the tone for the entire organization. If he or she is a brand skeptic, it will be difficult for the organization to develop and leverage the brand. But if the CEO views the brand as one of the organization's most valuable strategic assets and a key tool for implementing the mission and achieving impact, then the brand can become a driving and unifying force throughout the organization. In all internal and external discussions, presentations, and communications, the CEO can seize on the opportunity to reinforce the essence of the brand, thereby contributing to building brand Integrity. The CEO can also make brand Democracy a priority, emphasizing the role of internal education and training and empowering brand ambassadors. Finally, the CEO plays a critical role in building brand Affinity, as the strength of personal relationships is an important factor in building organizational partners. If you are the CEO of a nonprofit, you are the brand steward, and we encourage you to build brand Integrity, champion brand Democracy efforts, and encourage brand Affinity.

The Role of Marketing, Communications, and Fundraising

Many of the marketing, communications, and fundraising executives with whom we spoke during our two years of research are already implementing aspects of the brand IDEA. Many of these individuals have been bravely promoting brand and the importance of brand management in their organizations despite the existence of brand skeptics and a lack of understanding and support. In many nonprofit organizations, marketing and communications staff have to counter the mistaken impression that focusing on the organization's brand is somehow in conflict with the mission and social impact of the organization. "To have a conversation about the brand seems frivolous to some people because we are in the trenches saving lives," explained Kate Roberts of PSI. But when the brand is seen as intimately connected to the mission, values, and strategy, conversations about how to shape and communicate the brand become fundamental and central to the work of the organization. If you are responsible for marketing, communications, or fundraising in your organization, take heart: your work is essential, and you are in the best position to help your colleagues throughout the organization build an understanding of what brand is, what it can do for your organization, and how it can most effectively be managed. You can use the brand IDEA both as an "on-ramp" for initiating a brand Democracy approach in your organization and as a framework for driving change.

The Role of Program and Field Staff

In many organizations, the program and field staff are the embodiment of the brand. How they talk about the organization and its programs, how they act, and what they do create experiences and perceptions that tie back directly to brand image. They are among the organization's most powerful and genuine brand ambassadors. They are also the internal constituents most closely connected to the work, the beneficiaries, and the partners. Program and field staff hold a wealth of important information and knowledge about the needs of constituents and the role and positioning of other actors in the field. They should be key participants in brand Democracy efforts and in defining, articulating, and communicating brand identity. If you are involved in program or field operations, you are the organization's brand ambassador, and your knowledge and know-how are vital to keeping the brand relevant and authentic. Speak up. Share your knowledge and your stories and actively participate in shaping and using your organization's brand to support and strengthen your work.

The Role of Volunteers

Some nonprofits rely almost entirely on an active group of volunteers who serve as board members and play operational roles throughout the organization. Others utilize volunteers for specific operational functions or activities. As with program and field staff, volunteers can play an important role in defining and articulating brand identity and serving as brand ambassadors. Many nonprofits have not fully captured the substantial value that their volunteers can bring. If you are a volunteer for a nonprofit organization, we encourage you to share your perspective and look for stories that capture the essence of your organization's brand. Ramp up your engagement and think of yourself as a brand ambassador and champion.

The Role of Funders

Funders can play a multitude of roles to strengthen the organizational brands of nonprofits and increase overall impact and capacity. Funders can encourage grantees to develop a clear mission, an articulated theory of change, well-defined positioning and differentiation, and an explicit brand management strategy. These efforts can reduce duplicative efforts in the sector and ensure that each organization is adding value in a unique way that meets an important and specified need. We described in Chapter Nine how foundations can play an important role beyond simply funding organizations, by bringing organizations together to work toward a greater cause and encouraging more brand Integrity, Democracy, and Affinity. If you are a grant-making organization, you can have a tremendous impact building the capacity and effectiveness of your grantees by promoting and supporting their use of the brand IDEA.

The Role of Individual Donors

Individual donors can also become active brand ambassadors and promote the organizations they care about. As a donor's role evolves with the power of social media, there are increasing opportunities to become engaged in the organization and ensure that it maintains a relevant, clear, and authentic brand. As a donor, share your perspective on what the organization means to you and think of yourself both as a financial and strategic supporter to help the organization stay relevant and maintain a strong brand.

The Role of Partners

This book has made the case that collaboration is the way of the future. Organizations that understand the concepts of the brand IDEA, particularly brand Affinity, can share these ideas with their partners and help move the current discourse to one that focuses on shared external goals and impact. As a partner, you can lead by example, demonstrating the effectiveness of partnerships in terms of creating greater overall value and exemplifying how brand can be leveraged in service of collaboration and social change. Being generous in the use of your brand and brand assets in service to a common cause can stimulate others and build cooperation. You will probably be surprised by how quickly partners will reciprocate and emulate your brand Affinity approach.

CONCLUDING THOUGHTS

These are exciting times for nonprofit organizations. As described in Chapter One, we are seeing social change and management theories emerge that make the brand IDEA framework particularly relevant and compelling for nonprofit managers today. The concepts of organizational porosity and open innovation suggest that in the future, none of us will be working exclusively in traditional organizations with only our internal colleagues. We will increasingly be accomplishing our tasks within fluid teams and networks where access to information, assets, and responsibility will be open and widely shared. Brand Democracy is a process that fits well with this new environment, as well as with the idea of exponential fundraising. The notions of collective impact, shared value, and nonprofit networking, as well as shifts in monitoring and evaluation, point to a setting in which big, bold external goals are shared by multiple parties who will explore new ways of working together to achieve impact beyond individual organizational abilities. Brand Affinity is an approach poised to leverage these shifts and opportunities. Leadership experts talk about self-awareness, authenticity, and the ability to be collaborative and inclusive as key characteristics of great leaders. We believe that these same characteristics also hold true for great organizations and that they are an inherent part of the fabric of the brand IDEA framework. Brand Integrity is rooted in these ideas of self-awareness and authenticity. Knowing who you are, what you do, and why this matters can help nonprofits gain the clarity and focus that translates into effective action.

Although the brand IDEA is in some respects a normative model, a new framework that departs from traditional brand management practices, it is also a reflection of what many nonprofit organizations are already currently doing to leverage their brand in service of their missions, and is therefore also a descriptive model. In talking with a wide variety of organizations during the process of researching and writing this book, we were motivated and inspired by the tremendous difference that these organizations are making. It is our sincere hope that the brand IDEA framework can help all nonprofit organizations maximize their impact and support the incredible work that individuals associated with these organizations are doing every day to make our world a better place. We look forward to seeing an increasing number of strong nonprofit brands. Thank you and good luck. You can do it!

REFERENCES

INTRODUCTION

Edelman. 2012. *Edelman Trust Barometer*. http://www.edelman.com/trust/2012/.

Kylander, Nathalie, and Christopher Stone. 2012. The role of brand in the nonprofit sector. *Stanford Social Innovation Review* 10 (2): 35–41.

CHAPTER 1

Austin, James. 2000. Strategic collaboration between nonprofits and businesses. *Nonprofit and Voluntary Sector Quarterly* 29 (1): 69–97.

Bartone, Paul T., and Linton Wells II. 2009. *Understanding and leading porous network organizations*. Washington D.C.: National Defense University Center for Technology and National Security Policy.

Bulloch, Gib. 2009. *Development collaboration: None of our business?* London: Accenture. http://www.accenture.com/SiteCollectionDocuments/PDF/Accenture_Development_Collaboration_none_of_our_Business.pdf.

Clay, Alexa, and Roshan Paul. 2012. Open innovation: A muse for scaling. *Stanford Social Innovation Review* (Fall): 17–18.

Dixon, Julie, and Denise Keyes. 2013. The permanent disruption of social media. *Stanford Social Innovation Review* (Winter): 24–29.

Hanleybrown, Fay, John Kania, and Mark Kramer. 2012. Channeling change: Making collective impact work. (Blog post). *Stanford Social Innovation Review* (January 26). http://www.ssireview.org/blog/entry/channeling_change_making_collective_impact_work.

Hirschhorn, Larry, and Thomas Gilmore. 1992. The new boundaries of the "boundaryless" company. *Harvard Business Review* 70 (3): 104–115.

Jayawickrama, Sherine. 2011. NGOs and social media: Early experiences and key lessons. White paper produced for NGO Leaders Forum, Hauser Center for Nonprofit Organizations, Harvard University, Cambridge, Massachusetts.

Kania, John, and Mark Kramer. 2011. Collective impact. *Stanford Social Innovation Review* (Winter): 36–41.

Kanter, Beth. 2012. Becoming a networked nonprofit. (Blog post). *Stanford Social Innovation Review* (August 30). http://www.ssireview.org/blog/ entry/becoming_a_networked_nonprofit.

Klugman, Barbara. 2009. *Less is more: Thoughts on evaluating social justice advocacy.* New York: Ford Foundation.

Martin, Roger. 2012. Opening up the boundaries of the firm. (*Harvard Business Review* case study). Available at http://hbr.org/product/opening-up-the -boundaries-of-the-firm/an/ROT154-PDF-ENG.

McCrea, Jennifer. 2010. Exponential growth through collaboration. *Exponential Fundraising* (April 29). http://jennifermccrea.com/2010/04/ exponential-growth-collaboration/.

McCrea, Jennifer. 2012. Expobit: 14 see and clear obstacles. (Blog post). *Exponential Fundraising* (April 23). http://jennifermccrea.com/2012/04/ expobit-13/.

McCrea, Jennifer. 2013. A course in exponential fundraising. http://www.hks .harvard.edu/hauser/cef/.

Nee, Eric, and Michele Jolin. 2012. Roundtable on collective impact. *Stanford Social Innovation Review* (Fall): 25–29.

Peloza, John, and Loren Falkenberg. 2009. The role of collaboration in achieving corporate social responsibility objectives. *California Management Review* 51 (3): 95–113.

Pohle, George, and Jeff Hittner. 2008. Attaining sustainable growth through corporate social responsibility. IBM Institute for Business Value. http:// www-935.ibm.com/services/au/gbs/pdf/csr_re.pdf.

Porter, Michael, and Mark R. Kramer. 2011. Creating shared value. *Harvard Business Review* 89 (1/2): 62–77.

Rugh, Jim. 2008. The Rosetta Stone of logical frameworks. Table compiled for CARE International and InterAction's Evaluation Interest Group. http:// www.mande.co.uk/docs/Rosettastone.doc.

Sabeti, Heerad. 2011. The for-benefit enterprise. *Harvard Business Review* (November): 98–104.

Schmitz, Paul. 2011. *Everyone leads: Building leadership from the community up*. San Francisco: Jossey-Bass.

Sprinkle, Geoffrey B., and Laureen A. Maines. 2010. The benefits and costs of corporate social responsibility. *Business Horizons* 53 (5): 445–453.

Urban Institute. 2013. Nonprofits. http://www.urban.org/nonprofits/.

Wei-Skillern, Jan, and Sonia Marciano. 2008. The networked nonprofit. *Stanford Social Innovation Review* 6 (2): 38–43.

Yankey, John A., and Carol K. Willen. 2010. Collaboration and strategic alliances. In *The Jossey-Bass handbook of nonprofit leadership and management*. 3rd ed. Ed. David O. Renz, 375–400. San Francisco: Jossey-Bass.

CHAPTER 2

Aaker, David A. 1991. *Managing brand equity: Capitalizing on the value of a brand name*. New York: Free Press.

Aaker, David A. 1996. *Building strong brands*. New York: Free Press.

Aaker, David A. 2004. Leveraging the corporate brand. *California Management Review* 46 (3): 6–18.

Adamson, Allen P. 2006. *Brandsimple: How to turn a simple philosophy into a powerful brand*. New York: Palgrave Macmillan.

Andreasen, Alan, and Philip Kotler. 2007. *Strategic marketing for nonprofit organizations*. 7th ed. Upper Saddle River, NJ: Prentice Hall.

Argenti, Paul, and Bob Druckenmiller. 2004. Reputation and the corporate brand. *Corporate Reputation Review* 6 (4): 368–374.

Arnold, David. 1992. *The handbook of brand management*. London: Century.

Atilgan, Eda, Serkan Akinci, Safak Aksoy, and Erdener Kaynak. 2009. Customer-based brand equity for global brands: A multinational approach. *Journal of Euromarketing* 18 (2): 115–132.

Austin, James. 2000. Strategic collaboration between nonprofits and businesses. *Nonprofit and Voluntary Sector Quarterly* 29 (1): 69–97.

Bedbury, Scott, and Stephen Fenichell. 2002. *A new brand world: 8 principles for achieving brand leadership in the 21st century*. New York: Penguin Books.

Benz, Matthias. 2005. Not for the profit, but for the satisfaction? Evidence on worker well being in non-profit firms. *International Review for Social Sciences* 88 (2): 155–176.

Bergstrom, Alan, Dannielle Blumenthal, and Scott Crothers. 2002. Why internal branding matters: The case of Saab. *Corporate Reputation Review* 2 (3): 133–142.

Bishop, David. 2005. Not-for-profit brands: Why are many under-utilized by their owners? Paper presented at the 2nd Australian Nonprofit and Social Marketing Conference, September 22–23, Melbourne, Australia.

Bryce, Herrington J. 2007. The public's trust in nonprofit organizations: The role of relationship marketing and management. *California Management Review* 49 (4): 112–132.

Campbell, Margaret C. 2002. Building brand equity. *International Journal of Medical Marketing* 2 (3): 208–218.

Cuesta, Carlo. 2003. Building the nonprofit brand from the inside out. Creation In Common LLC. http://www.ashanet.org/centralnj/conference/2007/docs/BuildingtheNonprofitBrand.pdf.

Daw, Jocelyne, and Carol Cone. 2011. *Breakthrough nonprofit branding: Seven principles to power extraordinary results.* Hoboken, NJ: Wiley.

Deatherage, Joleen. 2009. The importance of nonprofit branding. *Philanthropy Journal* (July 24). http://www.philanthropyjournal.org/resources/marketingcommunications/importance-nonprofit-branding.

Ellis, K. 2004. Protecting your brand. *Franchising World* 36 (8): 18–20.

Fletcher, Winston. 2002. Cross-border consistency is a positive sign for trusted brands. *Marketing* (March 14): 18–19.

Foreman, Karen. 1999. Evolving global structures and the challenges facing international relief and development organizations. *Nonprofit and Voluntary Sector Quarterly* 28 (1): 178–197.

Fournier, Susan. 1998. Consumers and their brands: Developing relationship theory in consumer research. *Journal of Consumer Research* 24 (4): 343–353.

Guzman, Francisco, Jordi Montana, and Vicenta Sierra. 2006. Brand building by associating to public services: A reference group influence model. *Journal of Brand Management* 13 (4): 353–362.

Gylling, Catharina, and Kirsti Lindberg-Repo. 2006. Investigating the links between a corporate brand and a customer brand. *Journal of Brand Management* 13 (4): 257–267.

Hankinson, Philippa. 2005. The internal brand in leading UK charities. *Journal of Product and Brand Management* 13 (2–3): 84.

Heberden, Tim. 2002. Brand value management: The Achilles' heel of many risk management systems. *Association for Financial Professionals Exchange* 22 (4): 58–62.

Johar, Gita Venkataramani, Jaideep Sengupta, and Jennifer L. Aaker. 2005. Two roads to updating brand personality impressions: Trait versus evaluative inferencing. *Journal of Marketing Research* 42 (November): 458–469.

Kapferer, Jean-Noel. 2002. Is there really no hope for local brands? *Journal of Brand Management* 9 (3): 163–170.

Knox, Simon, and David Bickerton. 2003. The six conventions of corporate branding. *European Journal of Marketing* 37 (7/8): 998–1016.

Kotler, Philip. 2000. *Marketing management*. Upper Saddle River, NJ: Prentice Hall.

Laidler-Kylander, Nathalie, and Bernard Simonin. 2009. How international nonprofits build brand equity. *International Journal of Nonprofit and Voluntary Sector Marketing* 14 (1): 57–69.

Laidler-Kylander, Nathalie, John A. Quelch, and Bernard L. Simonin. 2007. Building and valuing global brands in the nonprofit sector. *Nonprofit Management and Leadership* 17 (3): 253–277.

Lencastre, Paulo, and Ana Corte-Real. 2010. One, two, three: A practical brand anatomy. *Journal of Brand Management* 17 (6): 399–412.

Letts, Christine W., William P. Ryan, and Allen Grossman. 1999. *High performance nonprofit organizations: Managing upstream for greater impact*. Hoboken, NJ: Wiley.

Liao, Mei-Na, Susan Foreman, and Adrian Sargeant. 2001. Market versus social orientation in the nonprofit context. *International Journal of Nonprofit and Voluntary Sector Marketing* 6 (3): 254–268.

Mitchell, Alan. 2005. The curse of brand narcissism. *Journal of Brand Management* 13 (1): 4–9.

Morrison, David E., and Julie Firmstone. 2000. The social function of trust and implications for e-commerce. *International Journal of Advertising* 19 (5): 599–623.

M'zungu, Simon D. M., Bill Merrilees, and Dale Miller. 2010. Brand management to protect brand equity: A conceptual model. *Journal of Brand Management* 17 (8): 605–617.

Nissim, Bill. 2004. Nonprofit branding: Unveiling the essentials. Guide Star. http://www.guidestar.org/DisplayArticle.do?articleId=833.

Ogilvy, David. 1983. *Ogilvy on advertising*. New York: Random House.

Oster, Sharon M. 1995. *Strategic management for nonprofit organizations*. New York: Oxford University Press.

Plummer, Joseph T. 1985. How personality makes a difference. *Journal of Advertising Research* 24 (6): 27–31.

Quelch, John, and Nathalie Laidler-Kylander. 2005. *The new global brands: Managing non-government organizations in the 21st century*. Toronto: Thomson South-Western.

Ritchie, Robin J. B., Sanjeev Swami, and Charles B. Weinberg. 1999. A brand new world for nonprofits. *International Journal of Nonprofit and Voluntary Sector Marketing* 4 (1): 26–42.

Roehm, Michelle L., and Alice M. Tybout. 2006. When will a brand scandal spill over, and how should competitors respond? *Journal of Marketing Research* 43 (3): 366–373.

Salamon, Lester M. 1999. The nonprofit sector at a crossroads: The case of America. *Voluntas: International Journal of Voluntary and Nonprofit Organisations* 10 (1): 5–23.

Sargeant, Adrian. 2009. *Marketing management for nonprofit organizations*. 3rd ed. Oxford: Oxford University Press.

Sentis, Keith, and Hazel Markus. 1986. Brand personality and the self. In *Advertising and consumer psychology*. Vol. 3. Ed. Jerry Corroe Olson and Keith Sentis, 132–148. New York: Praeger.

Thompson, Craig J., Aric Rindfleisch, and Zeynep Arsel. 2006. Emotional branding and the strategic value of the doppelgänger brand image. *Journal of Marketing* 70 (1): 50–64.

CHAPTER 3

Bergstrom, Alan, Danielle Blumenthal, and Scott Crothers. 2002. Why internal branding matters: The case of Saab. *Corporate Reputation Review* 2 (3): 133–142.

Bobula, Jessica. 2005. Internal branding becomes a hot topic for b-to-b. *Business to Business* 90 (11): 6.

Brest, Paul. 2010. The power of theories of change. *Stanford Social Innovation Review* 8 (2): 47–51.

Burmann, Christoph, and Sabrina Zeplin. 2005. Building brand commitment: A behavioral approach to internal brand management. *Journal of Brand Management* 12 (4): 279–300.

Foreman, Karen. 1999. Evolving global structures and the challenges facing international relief and development organizations. *Nonprofit and Voluntary Sector Quarterly* 28: 178–197.

Grossman, Allen, and Arthur McCaffrey. 2001. (Rev. ed. 2010). Jumpstart. Harvard Business School case study no. 301037-PDF-ENG. Watertown, MA: Harvard Business School Publishing.

Ries, Al, and Jack Trout. 2001. *Positioning: The battle for your mind.* New York: McGraw-Hill.

Sargeant, Adrian, and John B. Ford. 2007. The power of brands. *Stanford Social Innovation Review* 5 (1): 40–48.

Thomas, John Clayton. 2010. Outcome assessment and program evaluation. In *The Jossey-Bass handbook of nonprofit leadership and management.* 3rd ed. Ed. David O. Renz, 401–430. San Francisco: Jossey Bass.

Vallaster, Christine. 2004. Internal brand building in multicultural organizations: A roadmap towards action. *Qualitative Market Research* 7 (2): 100–113.

CHAPTER 4

Jayawickrama, Sherine. 2011. Embracing DNA, expanding horizons: The panda turns fifty. Hauser Center for Nonprofit Organizations, Harvard University. http://www.hks.harvard.edu/hauser/role-of-brand/.

Stone, Christopher. 2011. Amnesty International: Branding an organization that's also a movement. Hauser Center for Nonprofit Organizations, Harvard University. http://www.hks.harvard.edu/hauser/role-of-brand/.

CHAPTER 5

Stone, Christopher. 2011. Amnesty International: Branding an organization that's also a movement. Hauser Center for Nonprofit Organizations, Harvard University. http://www.hks.harvard.edu/hauser/role-of-brand/.

CHAPTER 6

Kylander, Nathalie. 2011. The Girl Effect brand: Using brand democracy to strengthen brand affinity. Hauser Center for Nonprofit Organizations, Harvard University. http://www.hks.harvard.edu/hauser/role-of-brand/.

CHAPTER 7

Kania, John, and Mark Kramer. 2011. Collective impact. *Stanford Social Innovation Review* (Winter): 36–41.

Kylander, Nathalie. 2011. The Girl Effect brand: Using brand democracy to strengthen brand affinity. Hauser Center for Nonprofit Organizations, Harvard University. http://www.hks.harvard.edu/hauser/role-of-brand/.

Oster, Sharon M. 1995. *Strategic management for nonprofit organizations*. New York: Oxford University Press.

Yankey, John A., and Carol K. Willen. 2010. Collaboration and strategic alliances. In *The Jossey-Bass handbook of nonprofit leadership and management*. 3rd ed. Ed. David O. Renz, 375–400. San Francisco: Jossey-Bass.

CHAPTER 8

Aaker, Jennifer, and Andy Smith. 2010. *The dragonfly effect: Quick, effective, and powerful ways to use social media to drive social change*. San Francisco: Jossey-Bass.

Harris Interactive. Harris Poll EquiTrend. http://www.harrisinteractive.com/Products/EquiTrend.aspx.

Jayawickrama, Sherine. 2011. Embracing DNA, expanding horizons: The panda turns fifty. Hauser Center for Nonprofit Organizations, Harvard University. http://www.hks.harvard.edu/hauser/role-of-brand/.

Kylander, Nathalie, and Christopher Stone. 2012. The role of brand in the nonprofit sector. *Stanford Social Innovation Review* (Spring): 37–41.

Oster, Sharon M. 1995. *Strategic management for nonprofit organizations*. New York: Oxford University Press.

Stone, Christopher. 2011. Amnesty International: Case study. Hauser Center for Nonprofit Organizations, Harvard University. http://www.hks.harvard.edu/hauser/role-of-brand/.

Twersky, Fay, Phil Buchanan, and Valerie Threlfall. 2013. Listening to those who matter most, the beneficiaries. *Stanford Social Innovation Review* (Spring): 40–45.

CHAPTER 9

Brothers, John, and Anne Sherman. 2011. *Building nonprofit capacity: A guide to managing change through organizational lifecycles*. San Francisco: Jossey-Bass.

Hammond, Darell. 2011. *KaBOOM! How one man built a movement to save play*. New York: Rodale Books.

Jayawickrama, Sherine. 2011. Embracing DNA, expanding horizons: The panda turns fifty. Hauser Center for Nonprofit Organizations, Harvard University. http://www.hks.harvard.edu/hauser/role-of-brand/.

Kylander, Nathalie. 2011. The Girl Effect brand: Using brand democracy to strengthen brand affinity. Hauser Center for Nonprofit Organizations, Harvard University. http://www.hks.harvard.edu/hauser/role-of-brand/.

Manzo, Peter. 2012. Branding social change? Review of *Uprising: How to build a brand and change the world by sparking cultural movements*, by Scott Goodson. *Stanford Social Innovation Review* (Fall): 15–16.

Moore, Geoffrey. 1999. *Inside the tornado: Marketing strategies from Silicon Valley's cutting edge*. 2nd ed. New York: HarperBusiness.

Shirky, Clay. 2008. *Here comes everybody: The power of organizing without organizations*. New York: Penguin Group.

Stevens, Susan K. 2002. *Nonprofit lifecycles: Stage-based wisdom for nonprofit capacity*. Wayzata, MN: Stagewise Enterprises.

CHAPTER 10

Speak, Karl. 1998. Brand stewardship. *Design Management Journal* (former series) 9 (1): 32–37.

INDIVIDUALS INTERVIEWED AND ORGANIZATIONS CITED

INDIVIDUALS

Abode, Philip, president of the board, Crossover Community Impact

Afkhami, Mahnaz, founder and president, Women's Learning Partnership

Allen, Wilmot, nonprofit adviser and founder, the Partnership for Urban Innovation

Baker, Kali, director of communications, Omaha Community Foundation

Balasubramaniam, R., MD, founder, Swami Vivekananda Youth Movement

Barlow, Joan, creative services manager, Robert Wood Johnson Foundation

Beeko, Markus, director of campaigns and communications, Amnesty International

Bell, Peter, senior research fellow, Hauser Institute for Civil Society, Harvard University, and former CEO of CARE

Benedict, Elizabeth, communications director, Social Venture Partners

Benito-Kowalski, Jennifer, director of outreach, Save the Redwoods League

Bildner, Jim, senior research fellow, Hauser Institute for Civil Society; adjunct lecturer in public policy, Harvard Kennedy School; trustee of many organizations, including Kresge Foundation and Nonprofit Finance Fund

Boyer, Mike, VP of strategic communications, Humanity United

Brandin, Pam, executive director, Vista Center for the Blind and Visually Impaired

Brew, Emily, former brand creative director, Nike Foundation (and Girl Effect)

Carty, Winthrop, executive director, Melton Foundation

Chanoff, Sasha, founder and CEO, RefugePoint

Childress, Angha, executive director, Barakat

Chukwuma, Innocent, executive director, CLEEN Foundation

Chyau, Carol, founder and CEO, Shokay

Davidson, Jill, director of publications and communications, Educators for Social Responsibility

Davis, Steve, president and CEO, PATH

De Graaf, Kees, management coordinator, Twaweza

Ding, Li, deputy director, Nonprofit Incubator

Dossa, Nooreen, communications manager, Educate Girls

Duffin, Peter, VP of brand and marketing, Lincoln Center for the Performing Arts

Dutt, Mallika, president and CEO, Breakthrough

Edmondson, Shannon, development and communications officer, Public Education Foundation

Emery, Pip, former head of brand identity/communications, Amnesty International

Ertel, Steve, director of media and external affairs, World Wildlife Fund

Ettinger, Alexis, head of strategy and marketing, Skoll Centre for Social Entrepreneurship, Oxford University

Fei, Deng, founder, Free Lunch for Children

Ferrell-Jones, Sylvia, president and CEO, YWCA Boston

Fuller, Lesley, funding, marketing and communications manager, Kibble Education and Care Center

Fulton, Katherine, president, Monitor Institute

Goddard, Anne, president and CEO, Childfund

Gutelius, Jeb, freelance nonprofit adviser

Hammock, John, associate professor of public policy, the Fletcher School, Tufts University

Hayes, Rachel, senior director, communications and community engagement, Oxfam America

Helfrich, Chris, director, Nothing But Nets

Hicks, Adam, former VP of marketing and communications, CARE USA

Hladin, Mihela, founder and CEO, Greenovate

Hogen, Robin, VP of communications, Robert Wood Johnson
    Foundation

Holewinski, Sarah, executive director, Center for Civilians in Conflict

Hurst, Aaron, founder and CEO, Taproot Foundation

Husain, Safeena, founder and CEO, Educate Girls

Jung, Julie, director of communications, University of Chicago
    School of Social Service Administration

Kuplic, Tom, president, ETO Consulting

Kurzina, Stephanie, VP of development and communications, Oxfam
    America

Lawry, Steve, senior research fellow, Hauser Institute for Civil
    Society, Harvard University

Letts, Christine, senior adviser, Hauser Institute for Civil Society,
    Harvard University, and Rita E. Hauser senior lecturer in the
    practice of philanthropy and nonprofit leadership, Harvard
    Kennedy School

Lloyd, Martin, marketing communications manager, Greenpeace

Manduke, Noah, chief strategy officer, Jeff Skoll Group, and former
    president, social service brand consultancy Durable Good

Marsh, Marcia, chief operating officer, World Wildlife Fund

McCrea, Jennifer, senior research fellow, Hauser Institute for Civil
    Society, Harvard University

McShane, Caitlyn, marketing and communications director,
    Opportunity Fund

Mehta, Shimmy, founder and CEO, Angelwish

Mendez, Steve, director of marketing, United Way of Dane County, WI

Morgan, Kerry, senior VP of marketing and communications, United
    Way of the National Capital Area

Ness, Alicia Bonner, former development officer, Girl Up

Novy-Hildesley, Will, nonprofit consultant and founder, Quicksilver
    Foundry

O'Brien, Julie, VP of communications and knowledge exchange,
    Management Sciences for Health

Parker, Stephen, leadership and organizational change expert

Paul, Mayur, head of communications and brand, HelpAge
    International

Payne, Christa, VP of external affairs, Public Education Foundation

Quelch, John, Charles Edward Wilson Professor of Business
    Administration, Harvard Business School

Reddick, Meghan, VP of communications, YMCA Canada

Roberts, Kate, VP of corporate marketing, communications, and
    advocacy, PSI

Ross, Holly, former executive director, Nonprofit Technology Network

Round, Cynthia, executive VP for brand strategy and marketing, United Way Worldwide

Saleh, Asif, senior director of strategy, communications, and capacity, BRAC

Sanchez, Laura, former senior associate for strategic communications and engagement, Living Cities, and current digital strategist, Atlantic Media Strategies

Schwartz, Beverly, VP of global marketing, Ashoka

Scott, Tom, director of global brand and innovation, Bill & Melinda Gates Foundation

Seckler, Kristin Suto, VP of branding and communications, Special Olympics

Sim, Jack, founder and CEO, World Toilet Organization

Singh, Ramesh, former chief executive, ActionAid, and formerly with Open Society Foundations

Srinath, Ingrid, executive director, Childline India

Stinebrickner-Kaufman, Taren, executive director and founder, SumOfUs.org

Stuart, Sara, director of communications and development, Union Settlement Association

Taylor, Jill, manager of foundation relations, American Academy of Pediatrics

Tellado, Marta, VP of global communications, Ford Foundation

Teriete, Christian, communications director, Global Call for Climate Action (and TckTckTck)

Thony, Sharon Lee, director of marketing, Girl Scouts USA

Thoren, Beth, director of communications and fundraising, Royal Society for the Protection of Birds

Tritch, Courtney, director of marketing, Northeast Indiana Regional Partnership

Tuzo, Alison, collection editor, Archive for Research in Archetypal Symbolism

Tyrrell, Shereen, former director of public education, Massachusetts Children's Trust Fund

van Dyke, Chris, former senior VP of strategic communications, World Wildlife Fund

van Riet, Marinke, international director, Publish What You Pay

Viatella, Kathy, managing director of programs, Sustainable Conservation

Vlachos, Panagiotis, founder, Forward Greece

Waggoner, Jenny, president, League of Women Voters of California

Wailand, Sybil, managing partner, Consumer Dynamics
Walker, Peter, director, Feinstein International Center, Tufts University
Wells, Matt, executive director, Diavolo Dance Theater
Wibulpolprasert, S., MD, senior adviser, Thailand Ministry of Health
Witter, Lisa, chief change officer, Fenton Communications
Wood, David, director of the initiative for responsible investment,
    Hauser Institute for Civil Society, Harvard University
Zaidman, Yasmina, director of communications and strategic
    partnerships, Acumen Fund
Zhou, Xian, founder and CEO, Buy42
Zobor, Kerry, VP of communications, World Wildlife Fund

ORGANIZATIONS

ActionAid
Acumen Fund
American Academy of Pediatrics
Amnesty International
Angelwish
Archive for Research in Archetypal Symbolism
Ashoka
Barakat
Bill & Melinda Gates Foundation
BRAC
Breakthrough
Buy42
CARE
Center for Civilians in Conflict
Childfund
Childline India
CLEEN Foundation
Crossover Community Impact
Diavolo Dance Theater
Educate Girls
Educators for Social Responsibility
Ford Foundation
Forward Greece
Free Lunch for Children
Girl Scouts USA
Girl Up
Global Call for Climate Action (TckTckTck)
Greenovate

Greenpeace
HelpAge International
Humanity United
Jumpstart
Kibble Education and Care Center
League of Women Voters of California
Lincoln Center for the Performing Arts
Living Cities
Management Sciences for Health
Massachusetts Children's Trust Fund
Melton Foundation
Monitor Institute
Nike Foundation (Girl Effect)
Non-Profit Incubator
Nonprofit Technology Network
Northeast Indiana Regional Partnership
Nothing But Nets
Omaha Community Foundation
Opportunity Fund
Oxfam America
PATH
PSI
Public Education Foundation
Publish What You Pay
RefugePoint
Robert Wood Johnson Foundation
Royal Society for the Protection of Birds
Save the Redwoods League
Shokay (a social enterprise)
Silicon Valley Community Foundation
Social Venture Partners
Special Olympics
SumOfUs.org
Sustainable Conservation
Swami Vivekananda Youth Movement
Taproot Foundation
Twaweza
Union Settlement Association
United Way of Dane County (Wisconsin)
United Way of the National Capital Area
United Way Worldwide
University of Chicago School of Social Service Administration

Vista Center for the Blind and Visually Impaired
Women's Learning Partnership
World Toilet Organization
World Wildlife Fund
YMCA Canada
YWCA Boston

THE AUTHORS

Nathalie Laidler-Kylander is a lecturer of public policy at the Harvard Kennedy School; a senior research fellow at the Hauser Institute for Civil Society, Harvard University; and an adjunct assistant professor of international business at the Fletcher School, Tufts University. She has been researching nonprofit brands since 2001 and has written extensively on the subject, including numerous case studies, a casebook, and several articles on nonprofit brand equity. Nathalie's prior work experience includes senior marketing positions in both the private and nonprofit sectors. She holds a BSc in biochemistry from Imperial College, London University, an MBA from Harvard Business School, and a PhD from the Fletcher School. Her research interests continue to focus on the role of nonprofit brands and the emergence of the fourth sector. Nathalie lives in Hingham, Massachusetts, with her husband and four children. For more information please visit www.nathalielaidlerkylander.com.

Julia Shepard Stenzel is a consultant to nonprofits and an active board member. Her work over the last twenty years has focused on strategy, policy development, and management systems. She previously worked for Kaiser Permanente; the World Health Organization; and Temple, Barker & Sloane (now part of Mercer Consulting). Julia received her BA from Princeton University and has an MBA from Harvard Business School. She lives in Orinda, California, with her husband and two children. For more information please visit www.juliastenzel.com.

ACKNOWLEDGMENTS

It is difficult to know where to start in acknowledging the contributions of so many individuals who have helped make this book a reality. Most important, though, is that this book would not have been possible without the generosity of more than one hundred individuals, engaged in some way with brand in the nonprofit sector, who enthusiastically gave their time, insights, and suggestions, sharing their stories and experiences with us between 2010 and 2012. Some of these contributors are highlighted in the book, but many, whose input was equally important, particularly in the early phase of the development of the brand IDEA framework, are not. Although they are too numerous to list individually, we are deeply indebted to everyone we spoke with and who was involved and supported our work. Many of you have become personal friends, and we hope you recognize your voice and wisdom in these pages. You are a true inspiration and the reason this book exists. Thank you!

In fall 2010, the Hauser Center for Nonprofit Organizations at the Harvard Kennedy School (now the Hauser Institute for Civil Society) was interested in conducting research for the Rockefeller Foundation on the role of brand in the nonprofit sector. Sherine Jayawickrama reached out to me (Nathalie) as someone who had been researching nonprofit brands for close to a decade, and I am so thankful she did. My thanks go to the Rockefeller Foundation and Zia Khan and his team for recognizing the importance of brand in the nonprofit sector and guiding our research, and later to Rob Garris for his continued support. Thanks also to the team of researchers from the Hauser Center: Sherine Jayawickrama, Johanna Chao Kreilick, and Alexandra Pittman (aka my brand sisters), who under the leadership of Chris Stone, former faculty director of the Hauser Center, developed the first iteration of the Role of Brand Cycle and the Brand IDEA, and in the process became my close friends and dearest colleagues. Their collaboration, research, and project management were invaluable. I am also thankful for the help of a number of research associates from the Hauser Center during this time, including Rahim Kanani, Natasha Sunderji, and Sonali Sharma.

In fall 2011, I was fortunate to come into contact with Eric Nee, managing editor of the *Stanford Social Innovation Review* (SSIR), who read an early version of the work and helped Chris Stone and me shape an article, published in the February 2012 issue of the SSIR, that subsequently became the basis for this book. My personal thanks to Chris Stone for being a wonderful partner and mentor and for putting up with our ping-pong matches and multiple edits. I am also thankful to Alison Hankey from Jossey-Bass, who reached out in spring 2012 and encouraged me to continue the research with the objective of writing this book. Thank you, Eric and Alison, for believing in the importance of this work and encouraging me to continue to research, write, and publish.

In summer 2012, I was at my twentieth Harvard Business School reunion, having lunch with my former classmates and silently fretting about how I was going to write an entire book in six months while teaching full-time and being a mom to four kids (three of whom are teenagers!), when Julia started talking about her interest in writing. The rest, as they say, is history. I could not have undertaken this book writing journey without Julia's partnership. Our collaboration has led to unanticipated adventures, a growing friendship, and this book.

Throughout fall 2012, we continued to talk to many practitioners who inspired us and helped us deepen our understanding of the brand IDEA in many different kinds of organizations. We give special thanks to Johanna Chao Kreilick and to Lauren Liecau for their interviewing skills. We also had help from research associates Nneka Jenkins, Ed Frechette, Anjali Fleury, and Sarah Glavey. During this phase, we turned again to the work of Alexandra Pittman and her thoughtful analysis of the results from the first phase of the research, and had the opportunity to present our work at several meetings, including the SSIR Nonprofit Management Institute, where we gained useful feedback from participants. Thank you also to the fall 2012 MLD 801 students at the Harvard Kennedy School whose term assignment was to use the brand IDEA framework to analyze a nonprofit organization of their choice. Research from the works of students Anahi Godinez, Ruixi Hao, Gareth Hitchings, Vince Lampone, Dayoung Lee, and Justin Pickard is incorporated into the book. We are deeply grateful to the brave reviewers of the early and rather bad versions of this book: Gisele Morel, Chris Letts, Sherine Jayawickrama, and Aviva Argote, whose suggestions were instrumental in improving the text. Thanks also to Beth Thoren and Sarah Glavey for their careful chapter-by-chapter review of a later, slightly better version and to Byron Schneider, Nina Kreiden, and Michele Jones of Jossey-Bass for their help in fine-tuning the final version.

Finally, we are very thankful for the support of our respective families, who will be rather glad that "the book" is done, and for the life-sustaining, morale-boosting power of chocolate.

INDEX

Page references followed by *fig* indicate an illustrated figure; followed by *t* indicate a table; followed by *e* indicate an exhibit